WISLEY
THE ROYAL HORTICULTURAL
SOCIETY'S GARDEN
Martyn and Alison Rix

WISLEY
THE ROYAL HORTICULTURAL SOCIETY'S GARDEN
Martyn and Alison Rix

In collaboration with
The Royal Horticultural Society

Colour photographs by W. Halliday FRPS
and Martyn Rix

Julian Holland Publishing Ltd
Somerset England

First published in Great Britain by Julian Holland Publishing Limited, 1989.

JULIAN HOLLAND PUBLISHING LTD
Ham Street
Baltonsborough
Somerset BA6 8QB

Designed by Julian Holland

British Library Cataloguing in Publication Data
Rix, Martyn
 Wisley: the Royal Horticultural Society's garden
 1. Surrey. Wisley. Horticulture. Organisations. Royal Horticultural Society. Gardens. Visitors' guides
 I. Title II. Rix, Alison
 914.22'162

 ISBN 1-871919-01-0 pbk

Typeset by Minster Typesetting

Printed and bound in Hong Kong.

Acknowledgements
We should like to thank all the members of RHS staff, both at Wisley and Vincent Square, who gave us help and encouragement in compiling this book. Special thanks must go to Audrey Brooks, Elspeth Napier and Fay Sharman for reading and checking the typescript; to Philip McMillan Browse for sparing some of his valuable time in order to explain to us his plans for the future development of the Garden; to Peter Barnes and David Pycraft for their helpful advice and anecdotes; to Harry Baker and Sheila Ecklin for their kindness in checking parts of the typescript; to Judith Jepson for her help in the library at Wisley, and to the staff of the Lindley Library at Vincent Square for their patience in dealing with our queries.

Illustrations
All the colour photographs, with the exception of those on pages 41, 42, 48 (top), 51, 54, 55, 68, 75, 77 (lower), 88, 99 (lower), 114 (lower), 115 (lower), 116, 118, were taken by Wilf Halliday, staff photographer at Wisley; we are most grateful to him for allowing us to choose from a wide selection. The remaining transparencies were supplied by Martyn Rix. The half-tone illustrations were drawn from a wide range of sources, including the archives at Wisley and the library at Vincent Square.

Dr Martyn Rix Educated at Trinity College, Dublin, Corpus Christi College, Cambridge, and the Institute of Systematic Botany of the University of Zürich. Botanist at Wisley from 1975-78. Martyn has led and participated in numerous expeditions abroad, looking at and collecting plants in countries including Turkey, Iran, Kashmir, Sri Lanka, Central Asia, The Caucasus, Japan, China and South Africa. He has been author and co-author of many books, including *The Art of the Botanist* (Lutterworth), *Water Plants of the World* (Junk), *The Bulb Book* (Pan), *Growing Bulbs* (Helm), *Shrubs* (Pan/Macmillan), *Roses* (Pan/Macmillan) and *Garden Open Today* (Viking). Author of a number of scientific papers and contributor to *The Flora of Turkey* and *The European Garden Flora*. Contributor to magazines including *Country Life* and *The Field*. Assistant editor of *The Plantsman* magazine.

Alison Rix Studied at Trinity College of Music, London. Assistant Editor to the RHS, where she worked on the *Wisley Handbook* series, from 1977 – 1986. She has travelled with Martyn to many countries, including Turkey, Kashmir, Central Asia, The Caucasus and Japan, and was joint editor of *Garden Open Today* (Viking).

Contents

Foreword

I am delighted to have been asked to write a brief foreword to this book; it is, in fact, two books – firstly, a history of the Society and of the garden at Wisley, both before and during the Society's tenure, and secondly, a guide to the garden through the four seasons.

Having been closely involved in both the day-to-day running and the long-term development of the garden, I can vouch for the fact that the marvellous displays of plants of all kinds to be seen at Wisley are the result of constant dedication on the part of many people. In addition to the staff at the Garden, many committee members give freely of their time and knowledge (and sometimes, also, of their plants or seeds) assisting the Society to maintain its place in the forefront of international horticulture.

Visitors to Wisley will notice that a number of changes to the layout of the garden are currently being made; some of these developments are the result, directly or indirectly, of the severe storm which swept across southern England in October 1987 – the damage at Wisley was immense, and a large number of mature trees was lost, here as in many other large gardens in the area. We at the Society hope that the result of these changes will be that people are able to see more of interest than ever before at Wisley, and in a greater degree of comfort.

I hope that this book will provide a lasting memento of Wisley to all those, from all corners of the earth, who visit our garden throughout the year.

C.D. Brickell, Director General
The Royal Horticultural Society

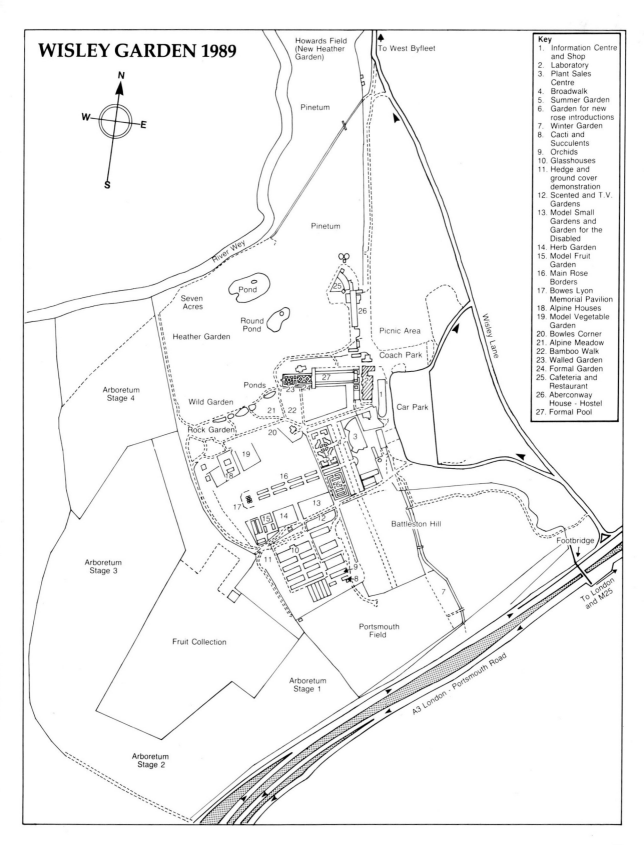

WISLEY GARDEN 1989

Key
1. Information Centre and Shop
2. Laboratory
3. Plant Sales Centre
4. Broadwalk
5. Summer Garden
6. Garden for new rose introductions
7. Winter Garden
8. Cacti and Succulents
9. Orchids
10. Glasshouses
11. Hedge and ground cover demonstration
12. Scented and T.V. Gardens
13. Model Small Gardens and Garden for the Disabled
14. Herb Garden
15. Model Fruit Garden
16. Main Rose Borders
17. Bowes Lyon Memorial Pavilion
18. Alpine Houses
19. Model Vegetable Garden
20. Bowles Corner
21. Alpine Meadow
22. Bamboo Walk
23. Walled Garden
24. Formal Garden
25. Cafeteria and Restaurant
26. Aberconway House - Hostel
27. Formal Pool

Howards Field (New Heather Garden)

To West Byfleet

Pinetum

Pinetum

River Wey

Pond

Seven Acres

Round Pond

Heather Garden

Wild Garden

Rock Garden

Arboretum Stage 4

Arboretum Stage 3

Arboretum Stage 1

Arboretum Stage 2

Fruit Collection

Portsmouth Field

Picnic Area

Coach Park

Car Park

Wisley Lane

Battleston Hill

Footbridge

To London and M25

A3 London - Portsmouth Road

Historical background

I N THE following pages we describe some of the chief events in the history of the Society; this may seem irrelevant to those who visit Wisley today. Yet it is only by a knowledge of the circumstances leading up to the acquisition of the garden in 1903/4 that the full extent of the Society's contribution to international horticulture can be fully appreciated. Naturally, the Society's garden plays a very important part in this work, yet few people realise that the RHS managed three other gardens before this one. In the design and management of these earlier gardens, one can see a microcosm of the fashions and fortunes of gardening from the beginning of the 19th century up to the present day.

Another aspect of the Society's contribution to horticulture is to be seen in the huge number of plants collected by men employed, or partly financed by, the Society; these were later introduced into general cultivation and became popular garden plants.

On pages 16 – 19 we give a brief account of the history of the garden at Wisley before it came into the Society's keeping. Prior to 1903, when it was generously given to the Society by Sir Thomas Hanbury, it was well-known as a private informal garden, full of interesting plants, belonging to Mr. G. F. Wilson, a local businessman. The fusion of these two strands of history can be seen in the garden at Wisley today.

The field on the south side of Battleston Hill was first planted in 1947, with a collection of ornamental cherries.

The Society until 1903

"That a society be formed to be called 'The Horticultural Society'.

"That the object of this society shall be to collect every information respecting the culture and treatment of all plants and trees, as well culinary as ornamental"

Thus proposed John Wedgwood, eldest son of Josiah Wedgwood the famous potter, in a letter to William Forsyth (commemorated in the genus *Forsythia*), gardener to King George III, dated June 29th 1801. The inaugural meeting of this Society was not held until 7 March 1804, at 187, Piccadilly, the house belonging to Mr Hatchard the bookseller. (A plaque in Hatchard's bookshop, still at the same address, commemorates the fact). In addition to Wedgwood and Forsyth five other men, the Rt. Hon. Sir Joseph Banks (President of the Royal Society), Rt. Hon. Charles Greville, Richard Anthony Salisbury, William Townsend Aiton and James Dickson attended, and founded a Society which was to be devoted to the improvement of horticulture.

By April 1805 a prospectus setting out the objectives of the society had been prepared by Thomas Andrew Knight, one of the original twenty-eight members of the society. Interestingly, he declared that

"Horticulture in its present state, may with propriety be divided into two distinct branches, the useful, and the ornamental; the first must occupy the principal attentions of the members of the society, but the second will not be neglected; and it will be their object, wherever it is practicable, to combine both."

From this it will be seen that the Society was conceived as a primarily practical and scientific association, on a par with the various societies for the improvement of agriculture which already existed throughout Britain. However, it was not long before the Society was also taking a leading role with regard to the introduction and cultivation of ornamental plants.

By 1818 membership of the Society (and, therefore, also its financial standing) had increased to such an extent that an acre and a half of land at Kensington was leased for use as an experimental garden. Here the Society's first gardener, Charles Strachan, started to make a collection of plants and trees, and carried out a series of vegetable and dahlia trials. In the next year, the Society purchased a house in Lower Regent Street, and this housed the office, a small library with its collection of botanical drawings, and a large meeting room where fruits, vegetables and flowers were exhibited at fortnightly meetings.

At about this time also, the introduction of new, chiefly ornamental, plants from abroad became an important activity encouraged by the Society. As early as 1817 an arrangement had been made with John Reeves, an employee of the East India Company, resident in Canton, by which he would purchase and send to England, plants and drawings of plants. (Many of the Reeves drawings depict camellias, chrysanthemums, paeonies, *Wisteria,* and other plants then unknown in the west). Other collectors employed by the Society during the 1820's included John Potts (China), George Don (Africa, S. America and West Indies), John Forbes (Brazil), John Damper Parks (China), David Douglas (America) and James McRae (S. America); between them, these men introduced many hundreds of trees and plants valuable in the garden, some of which can be seen growing today at Wisley e.g. *Pseudotsuga menziesii,* the Douglas Fir, and *Limnanthes douglasii* introduced by David Douglas, and *Camellia reticulata* first sent to Britain by John Parks; Parks also introduced the yellow tea-scented China rose which bore his name; it is now probably extinct in gardens in England, but has left its mark in its progeny, such as 'Gloire de Dijon'. His other Chinese garden rose, *R.banksiae* 'Lutea', has proved longer-lasting and can be seen on the walls of the laboratory at Wisley.

Always ambitious when it came to gardens, the Council of the Society soon decided that its plot at Kensington was too small for all the work that it wished to carry out. Encouraged by (erroneous!) reports that the Government might give some financial assistance to the Society, a committee was formed to seek out a suitable site for a larger garden at a convenient proximity to London. An advertisement was placed in the newspapers and, as a result, thirty-three acres of land were leased from the Duke of Devonshire at Chiswick. Plans for the layout of the new garden were prepared, and in February 1822 Mr (later Dr) John Lindley was appointed Assistant Secretary of the garden. By 1823 the original little garden had been given up, and the new one was laid out with about half the area devoted to the cultivation of fruit and vegetables, and the rest to ornamental plants. The variety of plants housed in this garden was incredible – for instance over 1,200 roses and 8,825 kinds of fruit were grown at one time – and the warm greenhouse was filled almost exclusively with plants sent back by the Society's own collectors.

Extensive trials of vegetables and fruit were carried out, and an ambitious start was made on an arboretum which was intended to include a specimen of every type of tree and shrub hardy in Britain. Another feature of the Chiswick garden was its training programme for young gardeners – rather unflatteringly known as 'labourers' – and this proved to be an extremely popular and successful venture. One of the most famous trainees was the young Joseph Paxton; his talents were soon spotted by the Duke of Devonshire – the Society's landlord and next-door-neighbour at Chiswick – and he became gardener at Chatsworth (the Duke's country house), where he was responsible for remodelling the gardens and for designing the great conservatory.

From 1833 until 1857 flower shows were held under canvas in the garden at Chiswick, and these were fashionable and well-attended occasions which sometimes brought in badly-needed revenue for the Society.

Introduction of new plants was continuing apace during the 1820's and '30s. David Douglas alone introduced more than two hundred trees and plants from California, and Theodore Hartweg, also employed by the Society, sent back large numbers of orchids and other tropical plants from America, as well as hardier ones, such as *Ceanothus rigidus* from S. California. As a result of this influx of tender plants more greenhouses had to be built to house them at Chiswick. *The Botanical Register* commented in 1839:

"All who are interested in the cultivation of exotic plants will be glad to learn that the Horticultural Society of London are about to erect a most extensive conservatory in the garden at Chiswick. The whole range, when executed, will be one of the most extensive in the world. No association of individuals has ever introduced so large a quantity of beautiful and useful plants into this country as have been procured by the Horticultural Society; but those plants have necessarily been confined very much to hardy species, in consequence of the want of extensive (sic-for the third time!) glass houses. It is now to be expected that greenhouse and stove plants will become a great object of attention; the effect of which will doubtless be to improve the ornamental character of tender plants in the same degree as that of hardy collections"

Unfortunately, in spite of this invaluable advance publicity, the 'most extensive conservatory' did not fully materialise – in other words, only part of the design was ever actually realised. Although a large range of glasshouses had been planned for the garden right from the start, the Society's perilously unstable finances always prevented the desired expansion from coming to fruition – however, in 1838 a committee approved the design for the new conservatory, and this consisted of a central dome and two wings. By 1840 one of the wings had been completed – the rest of the design was never enacted. Plant collecting continued, and after the signing of the Treaty of Nanking in 1842, it was decided that it would be *"advisable that the Horticultural Society immediately avail itself of the opportunity thus offered for the introduction to Great Britain of the useful and ornamental plants of that immense Empire"*. As a result Robert Fortune, previously in charge of the hot-house department at Chiswick, was despatched to China, armed with copious instructions from John Reeves (see page 10). Amongst his orders was the admonition to *"bear in mind that hardy plants are of the first importance to the Society, and that the value of the plants diminishes as the heat required to cultivate them is increased. Aquatics, Orchidaceae, or plants producing very handsome flowers are the only exception to this rule"*. Fortune did not return to England until 1846, having in the meantime sent home many fine plants, the majority of which are well-known and still popular today e.g. *Lonicera fragrantissimum, Weigela florida, Jasminum nudiflorum* and so on.

The 1850's were a time of extreme financial stringency for the Society, and many economies had to be made. The house in Regent Street was sold, and the office was moved to two rooms in St Martin's Place, near Trafalgar Square. Most of the magnificent library was dispersed, and, sadly, more than 1,500 original botanical drawings (including many of those commissioned in China by Reeves) were sold at Sotheby's, where they fetched £70, the highest price reached by any lot. (To put the anxious reader's mind at rest, we are happy to report that five volumes of the drawings were returned to the library in 1936, as part of a large bequest by Reginald Cory, and a further three volumes were bought back by the Society in 1953). Ironically, it was also realised that due to the proximity of the garden at Kew (itself in dire straits a few years earlier, and largely saved for the nation by the Horticultural Society) *"accessible as it is by railway and water, and with whose attractions it is hopeless to contend"* the Society's garden at Chiswick was annually becoming less popular with visitors. As the garden was also the greatest consumer of the Society's limited funds, it was decided that expenses must be reduced and that the garden should become less of a showplace and concentrate more on experimental work. To this end many

The vinery at Chiswick, formerly the conservatory.

greenhouse and tender plants were sold, duplicated fruit trees disposed of, and the large conservatory converted into a vinery. Trials of fruit and vegetables were set up, and many of the Fellows applauded this as a return to what they saw as the true work of the Society.

In March 1858 the Prince Consort was elected President, replacing the Duke of Devonshire, who had died two months earlier. Prince Albert's patronage marked an upturn in the fortunes of the Society, although not with immediate effect. At the beginning of 1859 the Society's financial affairs were still far from satisfactory, to the extent that some pessimistic Fellows found the whole position so depressing that they urged dissolution as the only possible course. Fortunately, however, the Society's secretary, Lindley, and Treasurer, Wilson Saunders, were more sanguine and persuaded the council to enquire of H.M. Commissioners for the Great (1851) Exhibition as to whether the Society might lease a site on their land at Kensington for use as a show garden. As a result of a meeting with Prince Albert at Buckingham Palace the Society launched an appeal for funds to enable them to go ahead with this scheme, and amazingly raised the necessary £50,000 by the end of the year. Queen Victoria and the Prince Consort both promised donations, and twelve princes and princesses were made Life Fellows; the patronage of the royal family was undoubtedly largely responsible for the extraordinary increase in Fellows that occurred during the 1860's.

Plans for the new garden, which was situated on 22½ acres south of the site now occupied by the Royal Albert Hall, were prepared under the supervision of the Prince Consort. On 1st May 1860 a meeting was held at the Museum of Science and Art at South Kensington, and here detailed designs for the site prepared by Mr W.A. Nesfield were exhibited. Under the terms of the lease the Commissioners undertook to *"surround the whole ground with beautiful Italian Arcades open to the Garden, and execute extensive ground works at a cost of £50,000, granting the Society a lease of the*

ground for 31 years, providing that the Society would at an equal cost lay out the Gardens and erect a Winter Garden at the north end".

Work on the new site was hampered by abnormally wet and frosty weather during 1860, but this did not prevent the Society from moving its headquarters from St Martin's Place to South Kensington in February 1861. In May that year a new Royal Charter was sealed, and from that time the Society became known as The Royal Horticultural Society.

The Prince Consort took great interest in the construction of the new garden and he performed the opening ceremony there on June 5th, 1861. His

The conservatory and winter garden at the Society's garden in South Kensington.

The entrance to the Society's garden in South Kensington. Note the words 'Royal Horticultural Society' – in May 1861, the year of the Society's removal to the garden at S. Kensington, a new Royal Charter was sealed, and from that time the prefix 'Royal' was used.

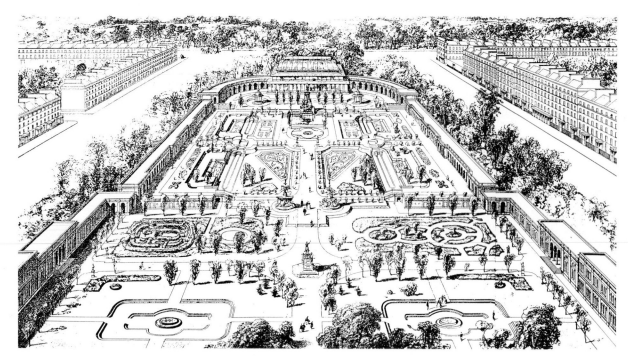

The Society's garden at South Kensington in 1862: Kensington Gardens and Hyde Park can be seen in the distance.

idea of the purpose of the garden, as outlined in his speech, bore little resemblance to that originally expressed by Thomas Andrew Knight (see page 10), as evidenced by his comment that *"unrivalled opportunities are here offered for the display of works of art and for the erection of monuments as tributes to great men".*

The drawing above gives a good overall view of the garden and some idea of its style can be had from this account by Andrew Murray in *The Book of The Royal Horticultural Society* (1863).

'...*we have front beds composed entirely of coloured gravels and Box, without any intermixture of bedding-out plants ... (they) are designed so as to represent natural objects, such as the Rose, the Thistle, the Shamrock and the Leek .... In addition to these ... there are seven large compartments in which the coloured gravel beds or paths form only portions of the compartments, and are intended to relieve their barrenness of flowers in winter, and combine with them in summer".*

This very formal garden was embellished with statues and fountains and a Fine Arts Committee and a Musical Committee were set up to oversee the arrangements. These cultural attractions, in addition to the horticultural wonders to be seen at the garden, and the interest taken by the Royal Family, helped to ensure that the garden became a fashionable meeting place.

In December 1861 Prince Albert died, and he was replaced as President, at the Queen's suggestion, by the Duke of Buccleuch.

The cost of finishing and furnishing the garden at Kensington had escalated until it was well above the original estimates. In addition, the Society was still running the garden at Chiswick, and carrying on valuable experiments there. At Chiswick, too, the thousands of plants needed for bedding-out at Kensington were raised, and rare plants that had been introduced by the Society's collectors were propagated and distributed to Fellows. Not surprisingly, therefore, during 1873 there was eventually a difference of opinion between the various factions of the Society – those who wanted a fashionable and elegant garden conveniently located in central London, and those who wished to support the small practical experimental garden at Chiswick. These differences of opinion, coupled with another financial crisis, led eventually to the termination of the Society's lease at Kensington, although the Society continued to have the use of the offices, council room and conservatory for its fortnightly meetings.

For some time the Society's Council had been contemplating moving the garden from Chiswick; the lease had only a few years left to run, and the worsening air pollution was becoming detrimental to the health of the plants. Hampered by lack of funds, the Society was unable to purchase a new site, and had also to curtail the work at Chiswick, reducing the area of land under cultivation from thirty-two to ten acres. Even so, thousands of plants were still grown, and in 1881 an exhibition was held in the great conservatory which attracted a large number of visitors, many of whom felt that this garden, rather than Kensington, represented the proper work of the Society.

In 1885 a new President, Sir Trevor Lawrence, was elected, and he immediately set to work to guide the Society back to its original path – the improvement of horticulture. Sir Trevor was a determined and interesting man; the son of Mrs Louisa Lawrence, one of the first female members of the Society, he studied medicine at St Bartholomew's Hospital and then spent ten years with the Army Medical Staff in India. He was a keen orchid grower and had a large collection of orchids in his garden in Surrey. He it was who instigated the Society's final removal from Kensington, to offices in Victoria Street, Westminster, a move which prompted the resignation of many of the "fashionable" Fellows who had enjoyed the amenities of the garden at Kensington. However, an equal number of keen gardeners from all over the country soon filled the vacant places, with the result that by 1900 the Society was once more in a position to consider expansion rather than retrenchment. It should perhaps be mentioned here that Lawrence was greatly helped in his work by the Society's Secretary, the Rev. William Wilks, Vicar of Shirley, Surrey, who bred the Shirley poppies and is commemorated by the wrought-iron gates at the entrance to the garden at Wisley today.

Although the arrangements at Victoria Street were reasonably satisfactory, many prominent Fellows, notably Baron Henry Schroder, felt that the next obvious step was for the Society to acquire a London base of its own; this, they felt, would be an appropriate way to celebrate the Society's centenary in 1904. A minority of Fellows felt that a new garden was a far more important priority, and at one stage, the Council went so far as to ask for authority to purchase land, first at Limpsfield, Surrey, and then at South Darenth in Kent; permission was not forthcoming, however, so attention was once again focused on the possibility of obtaining a new hall, office and library in London. The construction of the present building in Vincent Square was largely due to the foresight and generosity of Baron Schroder, who bought a 999 year lease on the site for the Society in 1902.

Despite the fact that interest now centred on the plans for the hall, the need for a new garden had not been forgotten. A committee had been formed to search for a possible site, but in view of the financial commitments already undertaken in London, it seemed unlikely that the Society would be able to raise sufficient money to purchase a garden also. Just when the Council had resigned itself to a long wait, a second generous benefactor appeared – Sir Thomas Hanbury KCVO, owner of the famous garden at La Mortola in Italy. On the 4th August, 1903, he attended a Council meeting and, to everyone's delight and amazement, offered to purchase and present to the Society sixty acres of land at Wisley, including the garden of the late G.F. Wilson; naturally, this offer was eagerly accepted, and by 9th September the formal transfer of the land had been completed. Now the Society would be able to celebrate its centenary with both a new hall and a new garden.

Wisley – before the RHS

Gardening in late 19th century England was much influenced by the ideas of William Robinson, inveighing against the artificiality of Victorian bedding – such as had been practised at the Society's garden at Kensington – and advocating in its place a totally informal style in which plants from all over the world were grown in as natural a setting as possible. Robinson's views were put forward in *The Wild Garden* (1870) and in numerous articles by him, and by Gertrude Jekyll, who added a fine feeling for harmonious colour schemes and simple but artistic planting. It was against this background that G.F. Wilson bought the estate known as Oakwood (formerly 'The Glebe') near Wisley in Surrey in 1878 and began to lay out his ideal garden. George Fergusson Wilson (1822 – 1902) was a London businessman and managing director of Price's Patent Candle Company, which had taken over the firm originally founded by his father; he was also a chemist with an inventive flair. Gardening, however, was his chief love, and one of his inventions was

An advertisement for 'Gishurst Compound', invented by G.F. Wilson, which appeared in the Programme for the Society's Summer Show at Holland Park in 1915.

Gishurst Compound, a soapy insecticide known to all growers of hothouse grapes, named after his house in Weybridge. Fruit growing was his first interest, and he was a member of the RHS Fruit and Vegetable Committee from 1862, and for two years the Society's treasurer. Lilies were a later speciality of his, and it was probably the soil and aspect of the land at Wisley, so suited to their cultivation, that appealed to him. At that time, the estate at Oakwood consisted of nearly sixty acres of mainly poor land, part rough grazing and heather moor, with some arable land, a birchwood, and an area of ancient oak forest, with small streams draining a bog.

Wilson developed about a tenth of the estate as garden, the remainder of the land, Glebe Farm, being let to a tenant farmer. He, like Robinson, favoured an informal approach, and he tended to site his plants where they would do best, having at the same time due regard for the natural features of the land, regardless of colour schemes; little was imposed in the way of design.

It was in the natural oakwood (which gave the estate its name) that Wilson made his famous wild garden. Amongst the existing oaks and birches he planted masses of rhododendrons and azaleas, as well as other flowering shrubs, conifers and herbaceous plants. He also established primroses, gentians, and numerous bulbs here, notably Japanese lilies, which, as mentioned above, were one of his great passions. One clump of *Lilium rubellum* was still growing happily in 1959, and there are now fine stands of his *Cardiocrinum giganteum* and of *Lilium superbum* completely naturalised.

To the south and northeast of the wild garden Wilson constructed pools, and these he filled with waterlilies, planting Japanese irises and *Gunnera* around the margins. Contemporary photographs show these areas, and the rustic bridge on which Japanese *Wisteria* was trained so that the long racemes could hang into the water, looking remarkably similar to today. This, in fact, is not surprising as the RHS Council decided that the Wild

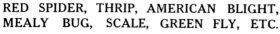

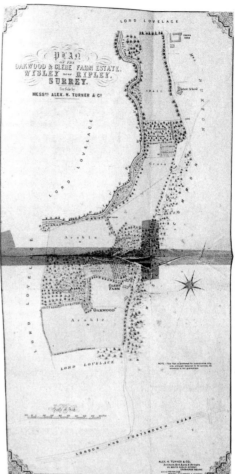

Garden and its immediate surroundings should, as far as possible, be preserved and continued in a manner which would have pleased Wilson.

The alpine meadow, by the rock garden, was another feature developed by Wilson, and it is spectacular in spring when covered with a mass of the little hoop petticoat daffodils, *Narcissus bulbocodium*, and in autumn with crocuses, and colchicums.

In addition to these features, there were at Wisley a kitchen garden, some fruit trees, and nursery beds. The buildings comprised a gardener's cottage (now known as Weather Hill Cottage, the curator's house), a thatched fruit room, a small farmhouse, a barn, and a few sheds.

Wilson died in 1902, and on hearing of his demise it was suggested by a member of the RHS Council that enquiries should be made as to whether the garden at Wisley was likely to be put up for sale. Presumably due to the Society's preoccupation with the construction of its new hall and offices in Vincent Square (see page 15), no more was heard of this idea until the next year, when Sir Thomas Hanbury made his magnificent offer.

"The tidings we have to convey to our readers will fill them not only with gratitude but also with surprise. Horticulturists in general, and the Fellows

The Long Ponds at 'Oakwood' (as Wisley was then known) in 1899. The plantings of Gunnera and Iris Kaempferi were made by G.F. Wilson and were still to be seen in the early 1950's.

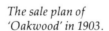

The sale plan of 'Oakwood' in 1903.

of the Royal Horticultural Society in particular, will rejoice that in SIR THOMAS HANBURY they have found a munificent and discriminative friend. He has presented to the Society the garden at Wisley, near Weybridge, so well known to a large circle of our readers as the creation of our late friend, MR. GEORGE WILSON."

Thus announced *The Gardeners' Chronicle* on August 15th, 1903, and it can be seen from this that the Society was lucky in that the garden was already well-known and popular amongst gardeners, a fact which must have helped to swell the number of visitors during the first year of RHS occupation.

Sir Thomas must be considered the greatest benefactor that the Society has ever had, and his gift of the land at

A view of the Wisteria bridge, date unknown, but probably during the early days of the Society's occupation of the garden.

Wilson's garden and gave it in trust for the perpetual use of the Society the deed stated that the Society should be allowed *"to use and occupy the Wisley Estate or such portion thereof as the Society may require for the purpose of an Experimental garden and the Encouragement and the Improvement of Scientific and Practical Horticulture in all its branches"*.

Wisley, in the summer of 1903, was described by *The Gardeners' Chronicle* as being

"....charmingly situated, quiet and out of the smoke of London. Even at Kew the trees suffer from the smoke and fog, so that in the future a new arboretum must be secured. Where better than Wisley? Wisley is reached from Weybridge by road, and there is a prospect that it will eventually be made more easily accessible by means of an electric tram along the Portsmouth road."

What would the writer of that article make of the A3 today!

Wisley could not have come at a more opportune moment. He was a member of a notable Quaker family of Shanghai merchants, and was keen on both botany and horticulture; his garden at La Mortola was, and is still, famous for its wonderful collection of plants, grown in a splendid coastal setting, and accounts of the garden there appeared in the RHS *Journal*. When he purchased

In March 1903 the lease and most of the plants at Chiswick were sold and the garden closed in May. S.T. Wright, who had been Superintendent at Chiswick since 1896, supervised the move to Wisley on 23rd April, and the Society began to take stock of its new property. Ironically, one of the positive features of the site was its rather poor soil and situation in a frost pocket – not immediately obvious as desirable characteristics in a garden! However, these drawbacks meant that plants cultivated at Wisley would not be grown under easy conditions – in common with the majority of private gardens – thus enabling the Society to test effectively the garden-worthiness of many kinds of plants. Trials of varieties of trees, fruits, flowers and vegetables were to constitute some of the main work of the Society, along with experiments in the cultivation and treatment of plants of horticultural interest. Other work planned for the new garden included the hybridization of plants and raising of new varieties, trials of horticultural machinery, composts, fertilizers etc., and the

Sir Thomas Hanbury, a keen gardener and the Society's greatest benefactor.

establishment of a school of horticulture. It was hoped that in due course a practical scientific department and a laboratory could be added.

The Chiswick metereological station, where records had been kept since 1825, was transferred to Wisley straight away, and daily records have been kept ever since (see page 112).

In spite of the lack of public transport and relatively small number of car-owning Fellows, the fame of the Wild Garden and interest in the Society and its new garden meant that more than 6,000 people visited Wisley during the first full year of RHS ownership.

The first construction work to be undertaken was a house for the Superintendent of the garden; to this was attached a small office and committee room. Work also began on a cottage for the foreman of the fruit and vegetable department, and two propagating pits, a melon house, fig house, vinery, peach and plant houses, and 400 feet of frames were also built. Some of the Wild Garden, which had become rather overgrown, was cleared, and the winter shelters (which had previously been thought necessary for these supposedly 'tender' plants!) for the rhododendrons and camellias were demolished. In the midst of this frenzy of activity, a large number of trees, shrubs and fruit trees – chiefly donated by leading nurserymen of the day – were planted and, as Harold Fletcher (sometime Director of Wisley) recounts

"... a Mr Todd presented a collection of vines for an outdoor vineyard which, although patiently continued for many years, failed to convince anyone but the donor that the production of grapes for wine was really worthwhile at Wisley".

The RHS at Wisley: 1904 – 1916

The years 1904 – 1916 were ones of great activity for the Society. On Friday 22nd July 1904 the hall and offices at Vincent Square in London were formally opened by King Edward VII (who also, with Queen Alexandra, became patron of the Society). Having at last found satisfactory and permanent head-quarters, the Society was now free to exploit the new garden to the utmost.

The Melon House, built in 1905; one of the range of glasshouses that used to stand in front of the lab. These glasshouses were demolished in 1969 to make way for the formal pool designed by Geoffrey Jellico.

Under the supervision of S.T. Wright, Superintendent of the Garden, the staff embarked on an ambitious programme of improvement and expansion, and were rewarded by a steady flow of appreciative visitors.

"There still appears to be some doubt as to the best means of reaching the Garden. To those who have to travel on the London and South Western Railway main line, Byfleet is the nearest station, being three miles away, and conveyances can always be found there ..... Fellows possessing motor cars find the Garden easy of access, as it is only about three hundred yards from the famous Portsmouth Road, one of the finest motoring roads in the kingdom. The average number of Fellows and their friends (visiting the garden) is about fifty a day – the maximum being over two hundred in one day – which proves that the splendid gift of the Garden by Sir Thomas Hanbury to the Society is well appreciated."

So said S.T. Wright, in a lecture given on July 18, 1905. In the same year, the building of the range of glasshouses mentioned in the previous chapter was completed, and a wide drive was constructed, leading to what is now known as Weather Hill Cottage. This wide drive was, and still is, the main entrance into the garden.

From the outset, the Society's scientific committee had been insistent that research should be undertaken at the garden, and this was started in a limited fashion. By 1906 the construction of a small laboratory had begun; built of brick, with a tiled roof, it housed a laboratory, a dark room, experimental greenhouse, office and storeroom. This building was used both for research work and as a centre for the students' lectures.

The new training course began in September 1907 under the direction of Mr F.J. Chittenden – a man destined to work for the Society for the next 44 years! The students paid an admission fee of five guineas for the two-year course, and received in turn instruction in practical experience in the garden, and lectures. The students were also able to attend the Society's shows and lectures in London and to study the experimental work and trials at the garden. The diploma granted by the Wisley School of Horticulture became a very popular and widely recognised path to employment in the gardening world.

At about this time also (no records were kept, and it is uncertain whether the first plantings were made in 1907 or 1909) work started on the Pinetum. Ever since David Douglas had been sent to western North America by the Society in 1825, conifers had been a special interest of the gardeners of Britain, for their ornamental and possible economic and forestry value. The polluted air at Chiswick had precluded the successful cultivation of many conifers, and the present Pinetum was one of the major new features formed when the Society took over the garden. The first plantings were on an extensive sandy area between the main garden and Wisley village. Some of the original trees still standing are the *Pinus* x *holfordiana* (see page 44), probably planted in about 1909.

Other notable specimens of rarities were *Pinus leucodermis,* the Bosnian pine (probably of the first stage of planting). The specimens of Leyland Cypress, x *Cupressocyparis leylandii,* although planted only in about 1928, have already reached around a hundred feet high. Some deciduous trees were originally planted among the conifers to relieve the

The site of the present Alpine Meadow, seen here some time before the First World War; the Rock Garden was constructed on the slope beyond.

heavy green colour; most have now been removed as they became over-mature, but fine Liquidambars and a large *Acer saccharinum,* silver maple, are among the most striking that remain.

In 1907, Reginald Farrer, the plant collector whose expeditions the Society had supported, published *My Rock Garden,* which gave added stimulus to the increasingly popular pastime of growing alpine plants. Farrer, Clarence Elliott – nurseryman and writer – and, later, W.E.Th. Ingwersen – who took charge of the Rock Garden at Wisley in 1917, and later founded the well-known nursery in Sussex – were all enthusiastic and articulate proselytisers of the glories of alpines.

"One is inclined to marvel at the tremendous growth that has taken place in the love of rock and water gardening in this country during recent years, and not only in this country but abroad, for it is a cult which has "caught on" in America and on the Continent". (J.R. Pulham in a lecture on August 13th, 1912).

It was obvious that the small area devoted to alpines which Wilson had laid out would need to be increased in size to satisfy the Fellows' interest in these plants. The Council decided therefore that another, much larger, rock garden should be constructed, and of the various plans submitted, that of

The original small laboratory at Wisley, constructed in 1906, and later incorporated into the new lab.

Students in the 'Botany Room' of the small laboratory in 1908.

Messrs Pulham, with assistance from Mr Edward White, a landscape architect, was selected. White and Pulham were fortunate in that the site was on a natural hillside, and there were already ponds at the base of the hill surrounded by well-established plants, and crossed by a bridge. It was decided that vistas should be created looking upwards from this bridge, the principal feature being a waterfall at the highest part, which would flow down through a series of small pools to the ponds at the bottom. As Pulham reported later *"The introduction of this waterfall and stream was, perhaps, a somewhat bold stroke, considering that the site appeared to be devoid of water with the exception of the lily pools already referred to. The designers of the scheme felt strongly, however, that it was very desirable, for many reasons, to introduce water, the chief reason being that, in their estimation, a rock garden without the damp and sedgy places which are necessary for the well-being of the many moisture-loving plants might well be likened to 'Hamlet' without the ghost".*

In the event, the waterfall and its attendant pools were constructed, an ingenious pump being used to take water from an old well at the bottom up to a large, newly-constructed reservoir at the top. The ground was cleared, vast quantities of Sussex sandstone imported from West Hoathly and moved to the various areas by means of a specially-built tramway. Great care was taken to place the rocks in almost the

same position as that from which they were quarried, thus giving the effect of natural formation. The stream, running from top to bottom of the rock garden, was lined with concrete, each section having a valve to enable it to be emptied and cleared out; other features incorporated in the scheme were a bog garden and a small moraine. Construction began in January 1911, and finished at the end of August in the same year; the high quality of the workmanship is evident in the fact that it was not until many years later that it was necessary for any major reconstruction to take place. On completion, the Society appointed a gardener specially experienced in the cultivation of rock garden and alpine plants, whose sole job was to plant up and maintain the Rock Garden. Many gifts of plants were received from such great gardeners as E.A. Bowles and Sir Frank Crisp. (For

'The Pines', built as a bothy for the student gardeners in 1911; the path in the foreground was known as the Lavender Walk.

details and illustrations of the Rock Garden as it is today see pages 74 – 76).

Other work carried out during 1910-12 included the construction of a house for the Director, and a new bothy for the students (now known as 'The Pines') next to what is now the formal walled garden. An orchid house was added to the existing range of glasshouses, and an alpine house, surrounded by frames, was also built.

During 1911, part of the garden now known as Howard's Field (see page 103) was planted up as an orchard, and a series of experiments on pollination and other subjects – such as the effects of summer pruning, and allowing grass to grow beneath young trees – was carried out.

Wisley Village

With the work of the Society at Wisley developing and expanding so rapidly, extra staff had to be taken on, and accommodation found for them. In 1915, therefore, five acres of land just north of the garden were bought, and the six cottages now known as 'The Square' were built. In 1919 the Society acquired an additional 160 acres of land, Deers Farm, adjacent to the northern end of the garden; included in the sale were several cottages, and in 1924 a further six cottages were built on this ground. Deers Farmhouse, now called The Lilacs, is occupied by the Fruit Officer. The small scattered village, with its beautiful 12th century church and village shop (now closed, but converted into flats for members of staff) today consists of about thirty RHS staff houses and twelve other houses, mostly privately owned. Over the years, more houses have been built – notably Chittenden Cottages (eight semi-detached dwellings constructed in the 1950's) – and the Old School House, now known as Orchard Cottage, has been converted into flats.

The New Laboratory

In 1913 the RHS Council set up a committee to report on ways *"in which the Society might assist and advance the more scientific aspects of Horticulture".*

The new laboratory under construction (photo probably taken in about 1915).

This committee duly concluded that it was necessary to increase the number of scientific staff at the garden, and that a new and larger lab should be built to house them. It was decided that the lab and garden should be overseen by a Director, with an Assistant Director responsible for the education of the students. The appointment of a chemist, entomologist, mycologist and trials officer was also proposed.

In January 1914 Professor Frederick Keeble, of Reading University, was appointed Director, and Chittenden became Director of the lab and head of the School of Horticulture. Work began on the new lab in the same year, incorporating the existing small building which had been in use for the last seven years (see page 21). The new building was designed by Messrs Pine-Coffin, Imrie and Angell of London, and constructed by Messrs Young and Son of Norwich. Made of narrow brick and oak half-timbering, and roofed with tiles collected from old country houses, the building has weathered well, deceiving many visitors as to its age.

By the time that this lab was commissioned, the RHS had taken to heart some of the lessons learnt from the management of its previous gardens; in short, it aimed to concentrate on practical horticulture and not to be diverted by the purely aesthetic, while

at the same time seeking to preserve the atmosphere of tranquillity and charm that was to be found at Wisley. In building a lab that looked like a country house, while at the same time providing efficient and well-lit accommodation for its staff, the Society showed imagination and good sense, and most visitors to the garden today would probably agree, as the RHS Journal opined in 1916-17 that *"it has been found possible to establish a great laboratory which does not detract from, but actually adds to, the beauty of the gardens".*

The building was constructed on three levels, due to the sloping site, and the surroundings were paved and terraced. The retaining walls were constructed of Sussex sandstone, capped with York stone, and planted with rock plants. Two water-lily ponds

The laboratory shortly after completion, in about 1916. Today the lab walls (see cover picture) are clothed with plants, which appreciate the sheltered sunny position.

A view of the glasshouses and the rock bank in front of the lab, in about 1910; the bank was constructed in an attempt to stop the erosion of the sloping land. The glasshouses were demolished in 1969.

were constructed, one of them being heated to enable the blue *Nymphaea stellata* to grow.

By the time of the lab's completion in 1916, the First World War had claimed the services of nearly all the members of staff at Wisley, and in some cases their lives also, with the result that most of the contemplated research work was not carried out until much later.

The RHS at Wisley: 1917 – 1931

At the height of the First World War, Professor Keeble was seconded to the Ministry of Agriculture as head of its Food Production Department. He resigned from the Society's services in 1919, to be succeeded as Director by Chittenden. In the same year, Lord Grenfell retired as President of the Society, and was succeeded by Lord

A field of lettuces growing on the site now occupied by the plant sales centre.

Lambourne. Meanwhile, Dr F.V. Darbishire, later chief chemist at the lab, was released from internment camp in Ruehleben, and started work on chemical analyses, mainly for wartime foods. Probably the most important piece of purely horticultural research work carried out at Wisley around this time was that by J.K. Ramsbottom, who discovered that hot-water treatment of daffodil bulbs would control eelworm; commercial growers had been losing thousands of pounds worth of bulbs through the depredations of this pest. Ramsbottom's work opened up a new area in the production of narcissus bulbs, and this success stimulated the Society's work as a scientific body.

Seven Acres

This was an area of rather rough pasture adjacent to the western side of Wilson's wild garden. Although a number of ornamental trees had been planted here during 1905, they had not grown well, and the ground had come to be regarded as useless for cultivation. However, by 1919, such a collection of new trees and shrubs had accumulated (mostly raised from seed sent back by Farrer and Forrest from Western China and Tibet) that lack of space caused a second assault to be made on this area. It was found that the problems encountered previously had been largely due to an underlying iron pan which had to be broken up before roots could penetrate to the moisture beneath. Once this snag was overcome the area was planted successfully.

Although Seven Acres was in a frost pocket, and had poor and rather dry soil, it proved ideal for hardier sun-loving genera such as *Buddleia, Berberis, Cotoneaster, Euonymus, Deutzia* and *Philadelphus* which had been sent back from China, though in lesser numbers than the then more popular genera *Rhododendron* and *Camellia* which preferred the sloping and partially shady conditions of Battleston Hill. The area was laid out with curving beds of mixed trees and shrubs, underplanted with trials of daffodils, surrounding a new, larger lake, which was dug in an area that had been a gravel pit. Many of the shrubs collected by Forrest and Farrer survived until the recent reorganisation of the area.

In addition, the discovery of small plants of ling scattered about in the grass led to the establishment of the Heather Garden (see page 121). As well as informal shrub beds, the area in front of the restaurant – at present lawn – was intersected by double herbaceous borders, as can be seen in the photographs on pages 30 & 32.

In 1922 the Society and the Ministry of Agriculture jointly set up a committee to administer trials of fruit for commercial growers. Part of the newly-acquired farmland was set aside for this project, which was, unusually for the RHS!, supported by an annual government grant. The National Fruit Trials, as they were known, were carried on at Wisley until 1960, when they were transferred to Brogdale, Nr Faversham in Kent, because of Wisley's liability to spring frosts.

1922 also saw the death of Wisley's popular and enthusiastic superintendent, S.T. Wright, who had done so much to transform the area surrounding Oakwood from farmland into an attractive and scientifically interesting garden. His successor, appointed in January 1923, was Arthur Simmonds, an ex-Wisley student, who became Assistant Director of the garden, before moving in 1925 to the Society's headquarters at Vincent Square, where he became Assistant Secretary and subsequently Secretary from 1956 – 1962. Simmonds was replaced at Wisley by Robert Findlay, previously head gardener at Logan and Castle Kennedy on the west coast of Scotland, and then Superintendent of the Royal Park at Greenwich.

In 1925 began the practice of opening the garden only to Fellows on Sunday afternoons from May to October. Over the years these times have gradually been extended so that the garden is open to members all day every Sunday.

Because of Sunday opening, on which day the lab was closed, a gatehouse was constructed by the garden staff, using

designs by the architects for the lab, Imrie and Angell. A uniformed Gate Attendant occupied this building, and presided over the Visitors Book, which, until 1962, was signed by all visitors to the garden.

The main entrance to the garden was also altered in 1925, and the wrought-iron gates through which everyone enters were hung to commemorate the Rev. W. Wilks (see page 66), who had done so much to help the Society.

In London, meanwhile, Lord Lambourne had laid the foundation stone of the Society's New Hall, in Greycoat Street which was formally opened in 1928 by the Princess Royal. In December of that year, Lord Lambourne died, and was replaced as President by Mr Gerald Loder, later Lord Wakehurst, an enthusiastic gardener and owner of Wakehurst Place, near Ardingly in Sussex, now owned by The National Trust, and administered by The Royal Botanic Gardens, Kew. Loder was particularly interested in trees and shrubs, especially rhododendrons, conifers, and New Zealand plants; his brother, Sir Edmund Loder, gardened at Leonardslee, also in Sussex, and was a keen hybridizer of rhododendrons. The influence of these two men did much to ensure that the new hybrid rhododendrons started to become exceedingly popular with Fellows of the Society.

In 1931 Loder resigned, due to pressure of work, and was succeeded as

The gatehouse, with uniformed attendant, in about 1947. Until 1962, all who came to the garden had to sign the Visitors' Book, kept in this lodge. To the left of the photograph can be seen the wrought-iron gates commemorating the Rev. W. Wilks, Secretary of the Society from 1888 to 1920.

Royal Horticultural Society.

Established A.D. 1804.

Incorporated A.D. 1809.

Offices: VINCENT SQUARE, WESTMINSTER, S.W 1.

Telegrams—"HORTENSIA SOWEST LONDON."

Telephone—No. 5363 Victoria.

PLANTS and SEEDS for DISTRIBUTION.

From the Society's Gardens, Wisley, 1919.

No plants will be sent to a Fellow whose subscription is in arrear.

NOTA BENE.—The correctness of the individual names given below cannot be absolutely guaranteed, as many of the plants are grown from seed and their identity has not yet been proved. The names are those sent to us with the seeds or of the plants from which the seeds were collected.

ABBREVIATIONS :—

A = Annual. G = Greenhouse. H = Hardy. S = Stove.

T = Tender, Winter protection.

N.B.—A Packet of Seeds counts as one plant.

The list of seeds and plants available for distribution in 1919; in this year seed was offered from Forrest's expedition to China.

President by the Hon. H.D. McLaren, later Lord Aberconway, another keen grower of shrubs, including rhododendrons. McLaren had been developing the garden at Bodnant in Wales inherited from his mother, Lady Aberconway, since the turn of the century; here he had planted a vast quantity of rhododendrons, magnolias, camellias, primulas, gentians and *Meconopsis*. He presented Wisley with a collection of Rhododendron species and a group of his own hybrids, which were planted on Battleston Hill (see opposite). He was also one of the first to recognise the significance of the new plants introduced from the collecting expeditions undertaken by Farrer, Forrest, E. H. Wilson, Rock and Kingdon Ward, and always encouraged the Society to support such expeditions, so that the garden at Wisley could boast a collection of the most interesting plants in the world. Such was Lord Aberconway's interest in the plants arriving in England that for a short time after Forrest's death in 1932 he himself employed Forrest's collectors, thus enriching British gardens still further. The wisdom of this was shown by the discovery and introduction of the excellent species *R. aberconwayi*.

One of the bonuses of the Society's support of collecting expeditions was to be found in the list of seeds and plants available for distribution to Fellows; the Society continued to send out plants until the beginning of the Second World War and still sends out vast quantities of seed today (see page 124). Some idea of the range of collecting activities supported by the Society can be seen from the fact that in 1929 the list included seed from no less than six expeditions.

At Vincent Square, meanwhile, it had been decided to create a new post, that of technical adviser, keeper of the library, and editor of the *Journal*; Chittenden (see page 20) was offered the job, and he moved to London in 1931, his place at Wisley being taken by R.L. Harrow, formerly Curator at The Royal Botanic Garden, Edinburgh. Chittenden had in fact been editing the *Journal* since 1908 and had also published numerous papers on subjects as diverse as mosses and fungi, and pollination in orchards. He edited the first edition of *Some Good Garden Plants*, published in 1929, a valuable work which described over two hundred plants *"likely to succeed in gardens in most parts of the British Isles"*. All the plants included had been given the Award of Garden Merit, instituted in 1921, the idea of this award being to distinguish those plants known to be of outstanding excellence in the garden. Most of the plants had been grown under trial at Wisley and observed for some time in the garden, and the results of these observations regarding the soil, aspect, and so on preferred by each plant, were noted.

At Wisley, a change was made regarding the students training course; the trainees were now paid, and spent the whole day working in the garden with lectures and lab work in the evenings. More students were taken on, and to provide the necessary accommodation, one of the houses in Wisley Village was converted into a hostel.

1931, however, was not an auspicious year for the Society, or for the country as a whole, as the effects of the economic depression began to tell. The number of Fellows fell, as did visitors to the garden, but fortunately there were no lasting consequences, and after 1933 the return to relative prosperity marked an increase in the number of Fellows which lasted until the outbreak of the Second World War.

The RHS at Wisley: 1932-1954

Under the directorship of R.L. Harrow the garden at Wisley continued to develop. Harrow had had the opportunity, when in Edinburgh, of growing many of the marvellous plants, including new species, that were being sent back by collectors such as Forrest. His skill as a grower of rare plants, often difficult to propagate, was to prove useful at Wisley.

In 1933 the Society exhibited, for the first time, at a flower show abroad. A co-operative exhibit, organised by the RHS, and consisting of new and rare plants introduced by British plant collectors since the turn of the century, was staged at the Ghent Floralies. The Royal Botanic Gardens at Kew, Edinburgh Botanic Garden, several nurseries, and a number of famous private gardeners also contributed plants to this exhibit, which attracted much attention from continental

gardeners. This was the only such venture during the '30's, but during the 1950's and '60's several exhibits were taken overseas (see page 34).

In 1934, timed to coincide with its Autumn Show in London, the Society held a conference on Apples and Pears. This showed the value of the work that was being done in the commercial fruit trials at Wisley – work that was to become even more significant during the war years.

During 1937 the northern slope of the recently-purchased Battleston Hill – a wooded ridge of high ground running parallel to the Portsmouth Road – was cleared, and planted with a collection of rhododendrons. The enthusiasm of the Society's President, Lord Aberconway (see opposite) undoubtedly played a part in this operation; he championed the cause of ericaceous plants of all

After the First World War a greater number of women were employed at Wisley, mirroring the situation in the country as a whole. Here, a group of women work in the wild garden in the 1930's – an area little changed from Wilson's day (see page 16).

The area of Battleston Hill known as 'The Dell', seen here in the late 1940's, soon after the Rhododendrons were planted.

types, and at a conference on ornamental flowering trees and shrubs held in 1938, he forecast the return of the camellia – as a hardy outdoor plant, rather than a greenhouse and conservatory subject (see page 19) – to almost universal popularity. Forrest had introduced several camellias from his expeditions, and one of the most successful of these (in English gardens) was *C.saluenensis*. Mr J.C. Williams of Caerhays castle, Cornwall, crossed this with *C. japonica* – which he had grown from Japanese seed – and the resulting hardy and beautiful hybrid was named *C.* x *williamsii*, of which numerous named clones are now available. The original *C.* x *williamsii* was a small-flowered single, later named 'J.C. Williams'. The best-known clone of the cross today is *C.* 'Donation', raised in 1927 at Borde Hill, by crossing Forrest's *C. saluenensis* with *C. japonica* 'Donckelarii'. In the following year, about an acre of land on the hill was planted with four hundred hardy hybrid rhododendrons which had been grown in a trial at Lionel de Rothschild's garden at Exbury. These grew well during the war years, and many were subsequently transplanted to other positions on Battleston Hill.

In the same year, 1938, Mr J.W. Blakey, who had previously worked for the great nursery firm of James Veitch and Son, was appointed Keeper of the Garden; he was tireless in raising thousands of plants from the seed sent back by Forrest and others. Some of these were grown on at Wisley, while vast quantities of surplus plants were sent out to the Fellows; the distribution of seeds and plants had always formed an important part of the Society's work, and although the sending out of plants was discontinued due to the war, seeds were sent out annually, a practice still continued today.

Wisley at War

The outbreak of war on the 3rd September 1939 not surprisingly affected the work of the Society to a considerable degree. Many of the London shows were cancelled, due to lighting restrictions, although later on in the war they were reinstated on a monthly basis; Chelsea Show was discontinued until 1947. Because of the risk of damage by enemy action, many of the more valuable books in the Lindley Library were housed at Wisley and Aberystwyth for the duration of the war. The staff at both Vincent Square and Wisley was greatly depleted due to the number of young men joining the forces, but despite this the garden was on the whole well maintained.

The Society played its part in the war effort to the best of its ability, one of its contributions being to organise a panel of voluntary lecturers and advisors (numbering 458 by February 1942) to help amateur gardeners increase their production of fruit and vegetables; they also advised the troops on the cultivation of their garden plots. A library of lantern slides illustrating the cultivation of vegetables was also built up, and the Society advised the Ministry of Information on the making of a series of films on the same subject. Many of these photos were eventually used to illustrate *The Vegetable Garden Displayed,* a booklet (later a full-size book) which was an immediate best-seller – over 50,000 copies were sold in 1942 alone – and is still in print today. In his foreword to the 1941 edition Lord Woolton, the Minister of Food wrote

"This is a Food War. Every extra row of vegetables in allotments saves shipping. If we grow more Potatoes we need not import so much Wheat. Carrots and Swedes, which can be stored through the winter, help to replace imported fruit.... I therefore welcome this booklet which encourages people to grow more vegetables".

Other wartime efforts at Wisley included the laying-out of a model allotment garden, the cultivation of vegetable seeds likely to be in short supply during the war, the collection of medicinal plants and their seeds, and – at the request of the Ministry of Agriculture – the undertaking of a series of tests on various chemicals designed to improve the keeping qualities of vegetables in storage, and other similar subjects. The age of entrants to the student-gardeners course was lowered to replace the older students who were nearly all serving in the forces.

Parcels of vegetable and flower seeds and bulbs were sent to the Camp Leaders in Prisoner of War Camps in Germany and Italy, and in October 1942 the Society reported in the *Journal* that *"Fellows will be pleased to hear that nine candidates from the Prisoner of War Camp, Stalag XXA, recently sat for the Society's General Examination (Seniors).."* (five men were successful). In the *Journal*, February 1943, the programme for the coming year was announced, giving a taste of the bleak times ahead.

"It is the intention of the Council to maintain all the privileges of the Fellows as are compatible with the prevailing circumstances and the directions that may from time to time be issued by the Government. Unfortunately... the Government has prohibited the despatch by train of flowers and of plants other than certain nursery stock. The Minister concerned, while fully recognizing the good work done by the Society, could not see his way to make any exception in regard to consignments for the Society's Shows. Moreover, the scarcity of fuel will prevent the growing of plants to flower early in the year. Under these circumstances such a full

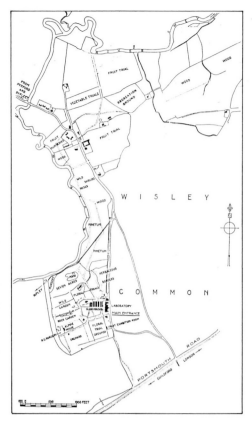

A map of the garden as it appeared in 1939. Note that Battleston Hill, and the area known today as the Portsmouth Field (Trials area) are not yet marked.

programme of monthly shows as in 1942 cannot be maintained. It is anticipated, however, that two shows for Fruit and Vegetables will be held.... Commencing in April, each month there will be a meeting of the Society at which Fellows and friends of the Society are asked to bring plants of interest, of recent introduction and the like, which will be on view to the Fellows and the public.... In order to encourage foc production, there will be staged smcl exhibits of fruit and vegetables from the Society's Trial Grounds and other sources.

At Wisley.... the testing of the seeds and vegetables acquired from the United States under the Lease and Lend Act will be undertaken for the Government in continuation of those successful trials completed in the year under review. Special attention will, of course, be paid to the Commercial Fruit Trials in view of the growing interest in fruit culture stimulated by the present conditions.

The standard collections of herbaceous and other plants will, as far as possible, be maintained so that after the war they may

Until 1971 a double herbaceous border, backed by yew hedges, dominated the area in front of the restaurant.

still be available for reference and for comparison."

Of course, it goes without saying, that none of this valuable work could have been carried out without the continued loyal support of the Fellows, most of whom, because of fuel rationing, were quite unable to visit either Wisley or the meetings in London; nevertheless, over 27,000 people gallantly continued to pay their subscriptions.

The Society's *Journal* was published almost as frequently as usual, rather thinner than previously, and including a section entitled 'The Wartime Kitchen Garden'. Every month a description of plants of particular interest to be seen at Wisley was included, enabling the armchair visitors to be kept in touch with the garden.

Chittenden, who had edited the *Journal* until 1939, had by this time begun work on the *RHS Dictionary of Gardening*, so Sir Daniel Hall became Editor until his death in 1942. He was succeeded by his assistant, Mrs Vera Higgins, who carried on until the end of the war, when she retired, to be replaced by Patrick Synge.

Wisley after the War
The war years had interrupted the work of the great plant collectors, and so it was an exciting moment for horticulturists when Frank Ludlow and George Sherriff were able to return to their hunting

grounds in Bhutan. After four years, in 1949, they sent back to Britain a large consignment of living plants by air – the first time that air freight had been used for such a vast quantity of specimens – and the result was that a number of hitherto unknown fine plants became well-established at Wisley, and in other British gardens. During the '40's and '50's other collectors – notably Polunin, Lowndes, Sykes, Stainton and Williams – visited Nepal. Expeditions in 1952 and 1954 were sponsored jointly by the RHS and the British Museum, and Sykes, who had just completed a two year course at Wisley, took part in both of these expeditions, introducing a number of new plants into cultivation.

The continuing introduction of rhododendrons, which had caught the imagination of the President (see page 27) and other gardeners with plenty of room, brought flowering shrubs into the height of fashion amongst the great gardeners. However, throughout the war, many of the great collections of rhododendrons, azaleas, magnolias, camellias and so on had become over-grown; some of these gardens were returned to their former glory – either by their owners or by the National Trust – while the burden of maintenance of others proved too great. Chiefly for economic reasons, the numbers of large private gardens, with their attendant staff, began to decline after the war, although a few new large gardens have been made since. In place of the grand houses and gardens, sprang up thousands of small houses, each with its own (usually tiny) garden, in which the owner/occupier was also the gardener. This new breed of amateur gardener was marked by a thirst for knowledge, and many turned to the RHS for help and advice; it is interesting to note that the Society's membership had risen rapidly after the War, to 49,586 by 1955 (just before the war the total had been 36,577).

In 1946 Mr Harrow, who had been Director since 1931, retired from Wisley and was replaced by Mr JSL Gilmour, formerly Assistant Director of The Royal Botanic Gardens, Kew. J.W. Blakey, the

Keeper of the Garden, also retired, and he was succeeded by Mr F.E.W. Hanger, previously employed at Exbury. Hanger was enthusiastic, energetic, and mad keen on growing rhododendrons, camellias, magnolias and other flowering shrubs; he is best remembered by *Camellia* x *williamsii* 'Francis Hanger', raised from *C.saluenensis* and *C.japonica* 'Alba Simplex'. This is one of the few white-flowered x *williamsii* cultivars, and it received an Award of Merit when exhibited in 1953.

Hanger at once set to work on the development and improvement of Battleston Hill (see page 27) which was for the next thirty-five years one of the most admired and most photographed areas of the garden. In an article in the *Journal* of April 1949, Hanger described some of the alterations that had been carried out at Wisley during, and immediately after, the war; in the autumn of 1946, for instance, two hundred trees and a hundred and fifty old stumps were removed from Battleston Hill, and hundreds of rhododendron and azalea species (many of them presented to the Society as gifts from the famous growers) planted. To Hanger's disappointment, the large-leaved *R.sinogrande* refused to grow on the poor sandy soil, and he wryly commented that *"the writer had found from experience that Wisley cannot be classified as one of the favourably situated gardens of England"*. Hanger also reported that the Pinetum, which during the war *"had (through shortage of labour) become rather wild and overgrown"* had been cleared, and additional conifers planted; the most notable of these were *"several of the newly – introduced Metasequoia glyptostroboides"*, whose hardiness at that time had yet to be tested. Other specimens of this tree, commonly known as the Dawn Redwood, were planted in the Wild Garden, and by 1970 (when it was last measured) one of these was found to be, at 56 feet, the second tallest in the country. Another development at Wisley during 1947-8 was the planting of a cherry garden on

the site of what is now the trials field. The Japanese flowering cherries were becoming popular at this time, but were poorly represented in the garden. To rectify this, three hundred species and hybrids were planted, including the famous 'Tai Haku', the Great White Cherry, rescued by Capt. Collingwood ('Cherry') Ingram from a garden in Sussex, and others introduced by him from Japanese temple gardens. Another minor alteration that was undertaken about this time was the tarring of certain roads and paths within the garden. This was done in an attempt to forestall a repeat of the damage done on July 16, 1947, when over four inches of rain fell

A view of the Broad Walk, leading up to Battleston Hill, taken in the early 1950's. At that time the area either side of the grass path was used to house the dahlia trials; today these beds are planted up as mixed borders.

On 16 June 1947 the garden was hit by a violent storm, which left a trail of destruction.

in an hour and a half, ruining many of the plants and washing away large numbers of labels. This flash flood, with its accompanying high winds and hailstones, caused considerable excitement amongst the visitors to the garden, the *Journal* reporting that *"Fellows sheltering in the Temperate House had to crowd for safety on the centre bench. Later they had to remove their shoes and stockings and wade under escort to the laboratory"*. Fortunately, no disaster of such magnitude occurred again, until the "Hurricane" of October 1987 (see page 42).

In 1951, the Director of Wisley, John Gilmour, resigned to take up an appointment as Director of the University Botanic Garden, Cambridge. He was succeeded by Dr H.R. Fletcher, who had previously worked at the Royal Botanic Garden, Edinburgh. Over the next few years, Fletcher and Hanger, the Curator, arranged the staging of some outstanding exhibits of plants such as rhododendrons, *Meconopsis*, lilies, and primulas at the Chelsea Flower Show, exhibits which acted as a 'shop window' in London for the garden.

In May 1953, Lord Aberconway, the Society's President since 1931, died; this was a great loss to the Society and also to the horticultural world in general, as he had been a man endowed not only with considerable qualities of determination and initiative, but also a great hybridizer and keen supporter of plant collecting expeditions. He was succeeded as President by the Hon. David Bowes Lyon, brother of the present Queen Elizabeth the Queen Mother. In his youth he had suffered from ill-health, as a result of which he was ordered by his doctors to spend some time working outdoors. He therefore went to work at Kew, where,

An aerial view of Wisley, taken in about 1950. Note the double herbaceous borders (see page 30) to the left of the picture, and the roofs of the glasshouses in front of the lab.

by a quirk of fate, his foreman was Frank Knight, later Director of Wisley (see page 34). His experiences at Kew were to stand him in good stead as President, giving him an understanding of those who practised horticulture professionally. He had inherited a fine garden, St Paul's Walden Bury, in Hertfordshire, and here he enjoyed growing a wide variety of plants, but especially roses, his favourite.

During the new President's first year of office, work was progressing on a new hostel to provide accommodation for thirty-six students at Wisley; the restaurant was also constructed at this time. The buildings were designed by Messrs. Sydney Tatchell, Son and Partners to conform with certain specifications laid down by the Ministry of Agriculture and Fisheries and the Ministry of Works.

1954 marked the sesquicentenary (150 years) of the foundation of the Society, and to celebrate the occasion a banquet was held at the Savoy Hotel, with a flower show and exhibition of the Society's finest books at the RHS halls. On the afternoon of 28th July, Her Majesty Queen Elizabeth the Queen Mother visited Wisley and opened the new students hostel, naming it Aberconway House in memory of the late President. She also planted a tulip tree in front of the hostel (where it still stands) and presented gold watches to two long-serving gardeners at Wisley, one of whom, Mr E. Smithers, had worked for fifty years in the Wild Garden – Wilson's original garden at Oakwood.

In her speech, the Queen Mother said:

"...*Your President has recalled that one of the earliest purposes of the founders was the training of young gardeners, and this need is certainly much greater today than it was a generation ago. Then there were up and down the country countless large gardens, each under the direction of a skilled head gardener from whom beginners might learn the science and craft of this most delightful pursuit, horticulture. Changing conditions have put an end to all but a few of them, but though gardens are*

smaller, they are certainly far more numerous. It is, I am sure, largely due to The Horticultural Society, for it is by their skill in growing and display both here and at Wisley and in Vincent Square that countless new doors have been opened wide.

The membership of the Royal Horticultural Society provides the best testimony to the intense and immense new interest that it has done so much to promote, and if gardens are to increase in beauty and science to assist discovery, opportunity must be provided for those who seek knowledge and experience. This splendid hostel will most admirably fill this great need, and I do not doubt the welcome it will receive. It is very fitting that it should bear the name of one whose contribution to The Royal Horticultural Society and to gardening was immeasurable."

In 1956 also, Dr Fletcher resigned from the directorship of Wisley, in order to

Aberconway House, the students hostel, and the restaurant under construction in 1953.

On July 28th, 1954 Her Majesty Queen Elizabeth the Queen Mother visited Wisley, and formally opened Aberconway House. In this picture she is seen flanked by her brother (also the Society's President) Sir David Bowes-Lyon and Harold Fletcher, at that time Director of the garden.

return to the Royal Botanic Garden, Edinburgh, where he became Regius Keeper. Fletcher was succeeded at Wisley by Mr F.P. Knight, a keen plantsman and practical gardener, who had worked in his youth at Werrington Park in Cornwall, where there was a fine collection of rhododendrons and other plants – some of them being introductions of E.H. Wilson, Forrest and Kingdon Ward. Mr Knight had been trained at the Royal Botanic Garden, Edinburgh, and followed this with six years at Kew (see page 33) prior to entering commercial horticulture. Possessed of abundant energy and skill, Frank immediately set to work on further improvements to both the garden and Wisley village – a task he was to continue for the next fifteen years.

The RHS at Wisley: 1955-1974

"1955 was a year of steady but unspectacular progress.... for the Society"; the number of Fellows was steadily increasing, and the shows were well patronized. At Wisley, the Society purchased more land lying between the garden and Wisley village, a number of the staff cottages were modernized, and in the following year two more cottages were built in the village.

Encouraged by Sir David Bowes Lyon, the Society (in co-operation with other British interests) staged exhibits at the Ghent Floralies international flower shows in 1955 and again in 1960, and also at shows in Paris in 1959 and Hamburg in 1963. This was a valuable opportunity to show off the type of plants – particularly woodland ones – that grew so well at Wisley and in other parts of England, and did much to encourage foreign visitors to British gardens. Francis Hanger, the Curator at Wisley (see page 31), played an important part in this work, designing the exhibit for the Parisian show, and supervising the packing, forwarding and staging of the plants.

The summer of 1955 was sunny and warm, and 149,925 visitors flocked to Wisley – nearly 10,000 more than in the previous year. Features of special interest during the year included the new plantings of Wisley-raised rhododendrons and azaleas on Battleston Hill and a small 'peatery' housing vacciniums, gaultherias, primulas and other woodland plants on the cool lower part of the north side of the hill.

The National Fruit Trials, which for so long had been carried out at Wisley, were by this time in the process of being moved to Brogdale, near Faversham in Kent, and the collection continued to be propagated for planting out at the new station.

Once again, during 1956, a record number of visitors to the Garden was reported at the Society's annual general meeting, a trend that has continued almost without a break until the present day. At that time, a large proportion of these visitors arrived during the spring, when the colourful displays on Battleston Hill were at their height. Many rhododendrons, especially species, which were well represented elsewhere in the garden, were moved to make way for more camellias (which, as predicted by Lord Aberconway, had become especially popular), magnolias, embothriums, primulas, *Meconopsis* species and other woodland plants. The Kurume azalea garden was by this time well established and Hanger continued his work on the hybridization of evergreen and deciduous rhododendrons. It is also interesting to note that, in 1956, experiments were carried out using mist-propagation technique – at that time a very new and exciting development.

During the 1950's the RHS also took its first faltering steps towards involvement with "the media"; in the Annual Report for 1956 it was stated that "The Curator continues to appear fortnightly with specialist teams from Wisley, on the BBC Gardening Club programme". Involvement with both radio and television has continued over the years, culminating in a series of television programmes, filmed at Wisley during the 1980's, entitled 'Gardener's Calendar'; a model garden was designed and planted at Wisley for use in this series, in which members of the RHS staff demonstrated garden techniques and practices.

Another innovation during the 1950's, was the construction of a small kiosk, by the main entrance to the garden, enabling visitors to purchase the Society's publications, including *"coloured postcards made from photographs taken at Wisley"*! (For details of the modern equivalent of this, see page 46).

One of the chief new attractions at Wisley in 1957/8 was the small area known as 'Bowles Corner', situated on the north-eastern slope of Weather Hill. This little garden was created in memory of E.A. Bowles, for long a pillar of the Society, a keen plantsman, and a vice-president and vice-chairman of Council for many years. Here a collection of the interesting or abnormal ('demented', as Bowles termed them) plants which had given him so much pleasure in his garden at Myddelton House, were established. Curiosities such as *Corylus avellana* 'Contorta', the corkscrew hazel, and *Galanthus nivalis* 'Scharlockii', the donkey's-ear snowdrop, may be seen today, as well as other plants – such as colchicums, crocuses and cyclamen – particularly loved and studied by Bowles. Although himself unmarried, Bowles had always been a great friend of young people, and had helped many of them to develop a career in horticulture; because of this, the RHS Council decided to establish (in 1956) a Bowles Memorial Scholarship, to enable Wisley student-gardeners, past or present, to travel abroad for the purpose of collecting plants for introduction into British gardens and/or for the study of horticulture. The entry requirements have since been widened to include horticultural and botanical students other than those at Wisley. In 1963 (see illustration) this scholarship was awarded to Brian Mathew (now a well-known authority on bulbous plants at

the Royal Botanic Gardens, Kew) and three other ex-Wisley students – David Baxter, Stuart Baker and David Pycraft (Horticultural Technical Officer at Wisley for the past 25 years) – enabling them to visit parts of Iran and Turkey. The early 1960's were particularly fruitful years for the alpine department at Wisley as, in addition to the Bowles' Scholarship expedition mentioned above, the Society sponsored other expeditions to the Middle East. In 1960, Rear-Admiral Paul Furse, recently retired from the Navy, set off on a two-month collecting trip to Turkey and Iran, his companion on this trip being Patrick Synge, Editor of the Society's *Journal*. A good collection of bulbs was brought back to Wisley from this trip, and future expeditions by Furse and his wife,

Members of the 1963 Bowles Scholarship Botanical Expedition to Iran and Turkey. From left, David Pycraft, David Baxter, Stuart Baker and Brian Mathew, with C.D. Brickell, botanist (wearing tie) and Margaret Briggs.

Ken Aslet and Christopher Brickell with bulbs from the Furse collection.

The plant pathologist, Audrey Brooks, checking the Furse bulbs for disease.

"The range of the mountains is his pasture, And he seeketh after every green thing".

Wisley continued to expand, with a total of 217,255 visitors to the garden in 1960. The increase in revenue meant that a number of improvements could be carried out, one of the most pressing of these being the installation of an additional water supply, with electrically operated pumps and a storage tank holding 60,000 gallons. Irrigation during dry spells had always been a problem in the garden, with its thin, sandy soil, and the new system meant that plants could be kept alive during dry weather, and even the lawns could be kept green. A new Model Vegetable Garden was laid out on Weather Hill (where it still stands today), showing how the amateur gardener could feed his family from a small plot managed efficiently.

In 1960 N.K. Gould, Botanist at Wisley since 1931, died, and was succeeded by his assistant C.D. Brickell, who was subsequently appointed Director of Wisley (a post he held from 1969 to 1985) and who is today Director General of the Society. Christopher Brickell took a degree in horticulture at Reading University and has wide-ranging horticultural interests; he has collected bulbs and other plants in Greece, Turkey and China and contributed to *Flora of Turkey* and *Flora Europaea*, in addition to writing a number of books. He also serves on a number of committees, including the International Commission for the Nomenclature of Cultivated Plants, and is a council member of the International Dendrology Society.

The following year, 1961, saw the untimely death of the Society's President, the Hon. Sir David Bowes Lyon, at the early age of fifty-nine. A popular and hard-working man, he was described by Lewis Palmer, the Treasurer of the Society and a close friend, as someone who despite *"his great connections and important activities, (he) would talk to anyone on level terms and with a touch of gaiety and humour that always warmed the heart"*. Sir David was replaced as President of the Society by

Polly, yielded further treasures, including several new species of *Iris*, and *Scilla* and *Muscari*; accounts of the expeditions in 1960, 1962, 1964 (when Afghanistan and Badakshan was also visited) and 1966 were published in the RHS *Journal*, and make fascinating reading.

The sheer quantity of bulbs arriving at Wisley meant that room had to be found for them, and raised frames – in which they could be planted out and studied as they came into flower – were built near the alpine house. The original alpine house and these frames have recently been replaced with two new houses (see page 70) on the same site. Whilst on the subject of plant collecting, we should mention here that Frank Kingdon-Ward (whose great contribution to horticulture was briefly mentioned on page 26), died in 1958 at the age of seventy-three. He had spent nearly fifty years in the Sino-Himalayan regions with only short breaks, and had collected an amazing number of beautiful and garden-worthy plants, including rhododendrons, magnolias, cotoneasters, viburnums, *Berberis*, *Meconopsis*, lilies, and gentians. The Society had supported several of his expeditions and raised seeds from them, and a plaque was put up in the entrance to the lab in his memory; this depicted *Lilium mackliniae*, which he discovered in Manipur and named after his wife, accompanied by a text from the psalm the 3rd Lord Aberconway, who had been a member of Council since 1958 and who was an authority on rhododendrons, magnolias, camellias and other shrubs, and whose father had been President (see page 26) before him.

Another death, that of Francis Hanger, occurred in the autumn of 1961. Hanger had a reputation among the garden staff as a hard man to work for, but under his stern control the garden flourished. He was himself a keen hybridizer and raiser of both Rhododendrons and Camellias, a skill which he brought to Wisley from Exbury, in Hampshire. His employer there, Lionel de Rothschild, had the reputation of being the foremost hybridizer of Rhododendrons at that time.

Hanger's death left vacant the post of Curator at Wisley. It was decided that the then Director, Frank Knight, would be able to combine both jobs, and it was not until 1980 that a curator was once again appointed at the garden.

All during the fifties and sixties Wisley continued to develop around the nucleus of Wilson's original garden, sometimes in a rather haphazard fashion, with fresh areas planted up to accommodate the influx of new plants, and features such as the model fruit and vegetable gardens created for the instruction of Fellows and other visitors. Russell Page, the well-known garden designer, highlighted this in his book *The Education of a Gardener* (1962) when he commented:

"The discussion between the adherents of "formal" and "informal" gardening still continues. This has always seemed to me a sterile argument, offering little but a display of partial understanding on both sides. For the "informalities" I would rather say that a garden which is after all a humanisation of nature and intended to be for "convenience and delight" needs, like all man-made structures, a framework. Its different parts need connecting in some kind of order.... In Europe the limits of dullness in garden design seems to me to be achieved in the decadent formality of the later followers of Le Notre; one glance from

the centre of the main axis of their dreary compositions is enough. There seems no point in setting out for a long and monotonous walk during which one will meet with no surprises and nothing of horticultural interest.

The informal "gardeners' garden" in its current form is an exact anthithesis. Its shapelessness and air of general confusion leaves a sense of disquiet which no number of well-planted episodes can quite dispel. Even the largest and finest are often ill-articulated. The Royal Horticultural Society's garden at Wisley comes to my mind as a series of charming incidents beautifully gardened but incoherent and unrelated to the site."

Perhaps it is no coincidence that various changes to the overall design of the garden were made over the next few years, culminating in the removal of the range of glasshouses which had cluttered up the ground in front of the lab for so long, and the building of an elegant formal pool in their place. This scheme was carried out in 1969 to a design conceived by Mr Lanning Roper and Sir Geoffrey Jellicoe, and it had the effect of opening up the west face of the lab, and providing a long view down towards the old potting shed and the formal walled garden behind. In the RHS *Journal* for March 1970 Lanning, who had been assistant editor from 1951 to 1957, described his plans for the treatment of the surrounding areas:

"At the far end, the potting shed is to be given a new look. It will be adapted to form an open loggia with water balconies, looking east along the canal and to the west over a walled garden, with colourful borders and a formal parterre with bedding schemes to replace those in the small beds along the cross-terrace walk. The brilliant carpet of wallflowers, myosotis, polyanthus and spring bulbs, followed by summer bedding, will make a pleasing contrast to the broad expanse of water in a predominantly green setting.

Hedges flanking a cross-path will bisect the frameyard, limiting the parterre and altering the scale, so that beds and borders more nearly approach the size of those we find in country gardens. We feel strongly that gardeners like to see schemes on a scale that they can adapt".

Most of these ideas were carried out, although some of the grass areas by the pool were replaced by paving, the pleached limes were removed after a few years because they did not grow satisfactorily, and the arches shown on the plan (see page 124) were never made.

The design and construction of the formal pool was regarded by most people as a successful project, although it has to be said that the same approbation was not accorded by everyone to the Bowes-Lyon pavilion, erected in memory of the former President (see page 32) in 1964. A competition was held in order to find the most suitable design, and ninety-eight entries were received; the assessors, appointed by the Society, regarded this number as *"highly gratifying, ... reflecting the interest aroused by the fusing of the two arts of the architect and the landscape architect."* The design chosen, a simple canopy of linked octagonal roofs on slender posts by Mr Derrick Lees, was considered by the assessors to be *"a dignified but light and elegant structure, combining the attributes of a memorial and a pleasant garden pavilion"* – the reader must judge for himself whether this description applies to the pavilion as seen in the late 1980's. The choice of a design using then modern materials such as perspex and steel was in line with the current fashion for modern architecture, but as with so many other buildings of the '60's the manmade materials have not aged gracefully, and with hindsight a more traditional design, such as the Italianate pavilion proposed by Clough Williams Ellis (the creator of Portmeiron) might have been preferable.

In some ways the 1960's were rather similar to the 1860's for the Society – in that it once again had the opportunities and funds to commission new buildings. In addition to the two projects described above, a new range of glasshouses was commissioned in 1968 from the Cambridge Glasshouse Company Ltd. to replace the old ones which had been demolished. Using aluminium alloy units similar to those of wide-span commercial greenhouses, the area under glass was increased from 18,000 to 25,000 square feet, and sophisticated heating and ventilation devices were installed. For further details of this area see pages 47 – 50.

During 1970 the land between Battleston Hill and the Portsmouth road was cleared of flowering cherries (see page 31) and developed to accommodate some of the floral trials which until that time had been grown in various areas scattered about the garden. During the next two years other trials were gradually moved to this area, underground water mains were laid on, and plots were defined with grass paths between. By 1975 the President, Lord Aberconway, was able to report at the Annual General Meeting:

"I said last year that most of the sites throughout the garden previously occupied incongruously by trials have been redeveloped as a part of the garden proper: the process will be largely completed this spring... the trials, concentrated on the Portsmouth Field, provide a colourful, varied and interesting spectacle throughout the year, not least to those motorists on the A3 who, now that the screen of trees has been cut down and road widening has started, have a splendid free view of this aspect of our activities: a view attractive enough, we hope, to have already induced some to visit the garden, but not a view so irresistible as yet to have caused any motoring casualties."

The Portsmouth Field today houses the trials of all hardy plants (with the exception of rhododendron and camellias) and vegetables, enabling visitors to compare many different cultivars at a glance. The work carried out by the Trials Department is described on page 98.

Due to soaring inflation and the collapse of stock market prices, 1974 was a bad year for the Society, financially speaking. Indeed, Lord Blakenham, the

Treasurer of the Society, reporting on the situation at the Annual General Meeting, said:

"Your Council has had to decide whether to slash the facilities which the Society provides for its Fellows or to raise the subscriptions. We could drastically cut the number of Westminster Shows. We could allow the Garden at Wisley and the service it renders to be run down. We could reduce the Journal *to four issues a year. After careful thought we decided that such action would be a retrograde step both in the long term interest of horticulture and of our Fellows.*

We must of course economise. This we are doing. We must also seek new sources of income.

For this purpose, the mail order scheme was launched last year. If we include the value of stocks we now hold available for future sale at no cost to ourselves we can claim a profit of at least £10,000 ..... Council has agreed to build a new Information Centre and selling area at the entrance of Wisley... Last year almost a quarter of a million people visited Wisley. I am certain that this will provide a very much needed amenity as well as a new source of income. However it will cost money – some £40,000 – to build as well as the finance required to stock the selling area but this will be a wise investment for the future."

Lord Blakenham was right – the Society's foray into commercial activities was, and still is, an unqualified success, and was to prove a major factor in securing the RHS's financial position, enabling it to remain the foremost horticultural society in the world. The income from RHS Enterprises, a trading company set up in 1975, which is wholly owned by, and covenants all profits to, the Society, helps to provide income (12% of the total in 1987) needed for the administration of the Society's work and the maintenance of the Garden. A branch of the Wisley Shop was opened in Japan in 1988, an event that would undoubtedly have surprised even Lord Blakenham!

The RHS at Wisley: 1975-1988

Despite the increase in subscriptions that had been necessary in the previous year, 1975 saw a rise not only in the number of Fellows but also of visitors to Wisley – a total of 289,692 people (the highest number ever recorded) by the end of October. The Model Vegetable Garden once again proved very popular, and the first of the small model gardens financed by the Stanley Smith Horticultural Trust was constructed during 1976, to a design by Mr G.K. Coombs, the Society's Garden Advisor until 1984. Other model gardens have been added since this time, the aim being to show how relatively small plots may be exploited to the full – whether to provide food for the family or as a relaxing place to sit quietly. As part of the Society's growing awareness of the needs of disabled people, a plot was developed in association with the Disabled Living Foundation, illustrating ways in which special features such as raised beds can be used to make gardening possible and enjoyable for those in wheelchairs. The most recent additions to this area are wildlife and scented gardens, reflecting the current interest in these ideas, and these were completed during 1988. Some of the special features (particularly trellis and a gazebo) constructed for the RHS garden exhibited at the Stoke Garden Festival (see page 41) have been used in these new gardens.

Various changes in the staff at Wisley occurred during the early 1970's, one of the saddest being the retirement of Ken Aslet, a popular character and great plantsman who had been in charge of the rock garden since 1949. Ken was interested in all manner of plants and selected several (which have since become popular) during his time at Wisley, including the lovely *Verbascum* 'Letitia', named after his wife. Nicknamed the 'Brain Drain' because of his fascination with drainage and water-flow (an occupational hazard on the large rock garden) Ken was never happier than when up to his elbows in mud; his successor in this capacity was John Warwick (see below), an ex-Wisley student who has himself now retired,

On March 10, 1978 the new Plant Sales Centre at Wisley was formally opened by Mr Percy Thrower, the occasion being witnessed by many members of the Press. In his speech, Mr Thrower remarked that he saw the Centre as a sign that the Society had *"appreciated the changing pattern of British Gardening."* He felt that the Society was performing a service in bringing to the attention of many gardeners some of the more unusual plants. There had been disquiet on the part of some nurserymen who had felt that retail sales of plants should be left to the trade, but in the end this resistance had been overcome, chiefly by adopting a policy whereby the RHS supplied propagating material to the trade who then produced and grew on plants for sale at Wisley. This centre (part of the expansion of RHS Enterprises already mentioned on page 39), in addition to boosting the Society's income also enables the RHS to distribute plants which are often in short supply; as Barry Ambrose (now managing Director of RHS Enterprises Ltd.) wrote in the *Journal* in 1978:

Her Majesty the Queen is introduced by John Warwick to the ancient Japanese larch on the Rock Garden.

"Over a period of time, our policy will be to introduce new species and cultivars and, in particular, to re-introduce many good garden plants which over the years have become scarce, either through streamlining or because of economic pressures within the nursery sector and other retail outlets, such as chainstores and supermarkets. Priority will be given to plants which have received awards either after trial at Wisley or the Society's Flower Shows."

On May 8, 1978 Her Majesty the Queen and His Royal Highness Prince Philip visited Wisley to mark the centenary year of the first recorded planting in the garden. They planted the first two trees in the new Arboretum, a pair of fastigiate purple beeches, *Fagus sylvatica* 'Dawyck Purple', either side of the entrance, and were conducted around the Garden by Lord Aberconway. Following a similar ceremony by her mother on the occasion of the Society's sesquicentenary in 1954 (see page 33) the Queen presented four long-serving members of the Garden staff with gold watches and certificates.

In June 1980 a new Curator, the first for nineteen years, was appointed; John Main, previously at The Northern Horticultural Society's garden at Harlow Car, filled this post until April 1988, when his place was taken by Jim Gardiner, previously Curator at the Hillier Arboretum in Hampshire. The Curator's job is to oversee all practical aspects of work in the garden maintaining it in good order throughout the year – no sinecure!

In 1980, Arthur Turner, the Superintendent of the Glasshouse, retired after twenty-three years at Wisley, and was replaced by Mr Ray Waite, formerly of Reading University. Mr Turner was one of the last gardeners of the old school, trained as a journeyman at many gardens including Exbury where, he used to say, they produced cherries the size of plums on Christmas Day. He had deep practical knowledge of all aspects of horticulture, and his grapes (which ornamented many Council lunches!) were surely the finest ever produced at Wisley.

1981 saw a threat to the peace and quiet of Wisley – already somewhat eroded by the increased traffic flow on the A3 road – in the form of a proposal to re-open the disused Wisley airfield. After a lengthy public hearing, at which the Society gave evidence and was represented by Counsel, the RHS Council's initial objection was upheld, to the relief of members. During the same year, work on the interchange for the M25 motorway was put in hand, and although this passed through land owned by the Society, the Garden itself was not affected. The advent of new and faster roads has contributed to the vastly increased number of visitors to the Garden in recent years; by 1982 the annual total was 410,000 and by 1987 this had risen to 615,000. As with all tourist attractions (for Wisley is "an attraction" in addition to being a scientific and botanically interesting garden), the difficulty is to prevent the sheer quantity of visitors from ruining the thing which they have come to see. To this end the Society has recently embarked on a programme of substantial capital expenditure in order to improve facilities at Wisley.

A large number of visitors come from abroad, either in groups, or as individuals, and for them, Wisley provides the outward face of the Society; many of these visitors are distinguished horticulturists or botanists in their own countries, and it is interesting to note that in 1981, for example, 3,092 visitors from 21 different countries were shown around the garden by the publicity officer (a post filled at that time by Mr John Clayton), while of course many other foreign visitors tour the gardens unescorted. Wisley has made substantial strides in the field of publicity recently, with a series of films, produced by Granada Television, entitled 'Gardener's Calendar' filmed in the garden and featuring members of the RHS staff. A special small garden was constructed for this series, and this can be seen alongside the other model gardens near the glasshouses. Another way in which the work of the Society has received exposure has been through its

Dr Igor Belolipov, Assistant Director of the Tashkent Botanical Gardens, Soviet Central Asia, admiring bulbs growing in the frames beside the old Alpine House.

participation in a series of International Garden Festivals, at Liverpool, Stoke and most recently, Glasgow. The aim of these festivals has been to revitalise areas of industrialised dereliction in major cities and to bring all facets of gardening to the attention of a wider public than heretofore; judging by the attendance figures reported, they would seem to have succeeded, at any rate, with regard to the second of these aims.

During the 1970's and 1980's research work of various kinds has continued to be carried out; one interesting example of this work arose as an offshoot of the Wisley airfield hearing mentioned above. This involved the im-plementation of a series of pollution experiments (in conjunction with Imperial College, London) using *Tagetes* as an indicator of pollution. Another project of interest has involved the breeding of a strain of red delphiniums (see page 42) by Professor R.A.H. Legro, who formerly worked for many years on this project at the Agricultural University at Wageningen, Holland. In addition to these projects, the normal range of experimental work has been undertaken in the Laboratory, under the

Some of the red delphiniums raised at Wisley by Professor Legro (see previous page).

The barograph reading for the week of the 'hurricane', showing the sudden drop in pressure. Wind speeds of over a 100 m.p.h. were recorded in the area.

supervision of the Senior Scientist, Miss Audrey Brooks, and this is described on pages 60–62.

In 1984 the RHS Council appointed an independent committee under the Chairmanship of Viscount Ridley to review the role, responsibilities, management and organisation of the Society as a whole and to report back to Council. After a number of meetings, both with RHS staff and members and with other horticultural organisations and establishments, the 'Ridley Committee', as it became known, published its findings and recommendations in 1985. In the section devoted to Wisley a number of recommendations were made, amongst them that a new Wisley Management Committee should be appointed – drawn from members of the RHS Council and other prominent horticulturists – whose job it would be to devise policies on which the future of the garden would be based. Changes

were also proposed to the horticultural training course, and this has now taken effect (see page 60). The most controversial of the Review Committee's suggestions was that the RHS should eventually move its headquarters (retaining an exhibition hall only) from London to Wisley; the committee felt that there would be several important advantages to both members and staff, but, to date, this scheme has not been implemented, and probably would not be, while the Society retains its present healthy financial position.

During 1985 work on the reconstruction of the Rock Garden – begun in 1981 – continued, and the old Alpine House and its surrounding frames were demolished. A new Alpine House and surrounding terraces was constructed in their place, fitted with an alarm system, sadly necessary in view of the thefts of plants from this area. In September of the same year Mr Brickell (see page 36) was appointed Director General of the Society, a new post carrying responsibility for all aspects of the Society's management), and his place as Director of Wisley was taken by Mr. P. Maudsley, formerly Horticultural Officer for the University of Durham. In early 1987 Mr Maudsley resigned from his post at Wisley, and he was succeeded in July of that year by Mr Philip McMillan Browse, formerly Director of the Saratoga Horticultural Foundation in California.

Friday, 16th October, 1987 is a date that will linger long in the memories of all who live in south-east England, for it was in the early hours that morning that the worst winds for several centuries, combined with saturated ground, created havoc over the landscape, blowing down around fifteen million of the oldest trees. Wisley was no exception, and tremendous damage was done to many of the garden's finest old trees. Battleston Hill was devastated as more than 80% of the mature oaks, pines and chestnuts were ripped out of the ground, and the Pinetum and Wild Garden were also badly affected. However, out of this disaster came some good for as the Director reported in the RHS Newsletter for May 1988:

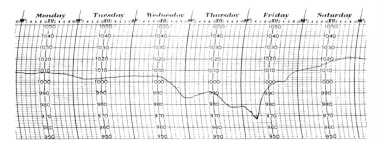

"Such extensive damage to the Garden necessarily caused much thought to be given to restoration and recovery. It became evident that the storm had sorted out many weak and senile specimens and, as on Battleston Hill, had dramatically altered the landscape. Such an impact gives us the opportunity to rethink completely and develop a new plan for much of the garden for the future. Wisley, after all, had never been designed in its entirety, it had simply tended to 'develop' and expand. Rather than replant and simply attempt to restore the landscape, we now have an opportunity to rethink the total function and development of the Garden for the next generation.

In order to work from a sound base we intend to work from scratch – albeit being constrained by many of the immutable structures and developments within the Garden. It is our intention to develop a garden which could withstand a million visitors a year in comfort."

Many of the recent developments at Wisley are described in the later chapters of this book, arranged by season, but of course it will be appreciated that the Garden is constantly changing. Our aim has been to give some idea of the multitude of delights to be found within this great Garden, and to enlighten the visitor (or armchair visitor) as to the work that goes on behind the scenes, both in the garden and the lab; we hope that you will enjoy the fruits of all our labours!

Baroness Trumpington, Parliamentary Secretary to the Ministry of Agriculture, seen here inspecting the storm damage on Battleston Hill. With her, from left, to right are: Jim Gardiner (Curator), Barry Ambrose (Managing Director, RHS Enterprises), The Lady Anne Palmer (who recently made her garden at Rosemoor, Devon, over to the RHS for use as a 'West Country Wisley') and the President of the Society, Mr Robin Herbert.

Weather Hill Cottage (formerly Oakwood, the oldest building at Wisley) narrowly avoided destruction from its mighty oak.

Winter

GARDEN VISITING does not immediately spring to mind as an idea for the entertainment of friends and family on a cold December afternoon. However, those who are eccentric enough to consider a visit to Wisley at this time of year will be pleasantly surprised on arrival at the Garden, and will not regret their choice.

Although certain aspects of Wisley, such as the collection of hybrid roses and herbaceous borders, are somewhat lacking in charm at this time of year there is plenty elsewhere to make up for it. By way of a winter tonic, we can recommend a visit to the large greenhouse, where one can wallow in the warm luxuriance of scent and foliage. The alpine houses are another refuge from the harsh realities of winter, and here one can see a marvellous range of early-flowering bulbs, such as crocuses, tulips, fritillaries and daffodils.

Signs of hope are to be found in the Wild Garden, where the hellebores often start to flower before Christmas, followed by the earliest snowdrops and dwarf daffodils, and in the Winter Garden, where the sweetly-scented Mahonias and Sarcococcas can be enjoyed on warm days. It is at this time of year that one realises just how valuable coloured barks and berries can be – in Seven Acres, for example, there are a number of trees and shrubs, such as *Acer rubrum* and *Cotoneaster*, that contribute colour to the scene.

Christmas Day is the only time that Wisley is closed to visitors, and on this day the birds have the place to themselves. A fascinating book, showing some of the wide range of birds to be seen in the Garden, has recently been published; written by David and June Elliott, and illustrated by Chris Howkins, it is entitled *Enjoying Wisley's Birds*, and is available at the shop.

Cones of Pinus x holfordiana, *a hybrid between* P. ayacahuite *and* P. wallichiana *named after Sir George Holford, the owner of Westonbirt Arboretum. There are two fine specimens in the Pinetum.*

The Plant Sales Centre at Wisley, which is operated by RHS Enterprises Ltd., the Society's trading company.

Entrance to the Garden

The entrance to the Garden is situated to the left of the large shop and Information Centre, operated by RHS Enterprises Ltd., a company whose formation and purpose is described on page 39. The shop, which contains the widest range of horticultural books in the country, as well as a selection of other gifts, is open every day of the year, with the exception of Christmas Day. Not surprisingly, therefore, it is very popular with visitors, especially in the weeks prior to Christmas.

To the left of the garden entrance is the Plant Sales Centre (see page 40), where a wide range of plants, both hardy and tender, together with seeds, gardening tools and other equipment can be purchased.

After passing through the entrance turnstiles, visitors enter the Garden itself through a pair of wrought-iron gates (see page 66), and can walk either up a short flight of steps on to the Main Terrace, or take the path in front of the Laboratory.

Main Terrace

In recent years there has been an excellent display of pansies in the circular beds either side of the path on the Main Terrace; small wonder that these plants are so popular when one realises that they often flower continuously from January to March, making a fine splash of colour. The type grown at Wisley are the 'Crystal Bowl' forms, which produce flowers of glowing jewel-like colours. They are often underplanted with tulips or other bulbs for spring display.

The Winter Garden

This is situated in a narrow area of woodland on the western side of Battleston Hill, bordering the Portsmouth Field, and contains shrubs and plants which are of ornamental value during the winter months.

Included here are shrubs which flower between November and March, such as the Mahonias, of which there are a number of fine specimens of different clones of *M.x media* Brickell, a hybrid between the very hardy *M.japonica* and the tender *M.lomariifolia*. This hybrid first appeared by chance among seedlings of *M.lomariifolia* sent to Russell's nursery at Windlesham, Surrey, by the Slieve Donard nursery in Northern Ireland, and was selected by Sir Eric Savill (of Savill Gardens fame). 'Charity' was the first to be named and is still the most popular of this group. Amongst others can be seen the newer cultivars *M.* 'Charity's Sister', 'Underway' and 'Lionel Fortescue'. Hellebores are also well represented, with the green-flowered *Helleborus lividus* ssp. *corsicus* making a fine show. One of the very early primroses, *Primula sibthorpii*, a species from Greece, produces its mauve flowers from December onwards: in all except its pinkish-mauve flowers, it is similar to the wild primrose.

Other trees and shrubs are included here on account of their attractive foliage or bark; a rare shrub for the curious is the hybrid between the deciduous *Parrotia persica* and the evergreen *Sycopsis sinensis*, aptly named x *Sycoparrotia semidecidua*.

The Glasshouses

Orchid and Cactus houses
In addition to the main glasshouse there are a number of smaller greenhouses, which house collections of orchids and cacti and succulents; these are situated between the main glasshouse range and the trials field.

The main glasshouse range
The main glasshouse complex was built in 1968, and is sited to the west of the trials field. It consists of a large Display House linked by a passage to three parallel pairs of smaller houses. The entrance is on the north – western side of the Display House, which is divided into three sections.

The central section is the largest, and

probably most impressive, and is designed to provide a temperate climate, with a minimum temperature of 10°C. It contains a central shallow pool in which a number of water plants (and goldfish!) thrive, the margins being planted with moisture-loving plants, such as the large white arum lily, *Zantedeschia aethiopica*, which flowers here in mid-winter, according to the season. During the winter of 1988/1989 there was an impressive group of *Calanthe vestita*, a cool-growing orchid which produces sprays of pink and white flowers alongside the naked pseudo-bulbs. Surrounding the pool are a wide variety of ornamental and climbing shrubs, many of which look surprisingly exotic, considering the relatively low temperature they require. Large-flowered *Hibiscus rosa-sinensis* hybrids and *Beloperone guttata*, the

The cactus house is situated between the main glasshouse range and the trials field. Cacti and succulents, such as aloes, are grown here.

The temperate section of the display glasshouse; amongst the lush foliage can be seen the red pendent flowers of Passiflora antioquiensis *and an* Impatiens.

Another view of the temperate display house, showing the small pool.

Shrimp Plant, which grows well planted in the open ground, forming a bush about 1.5 metres high, are notable here. Also of interest in early January are *Jacobinia pauciflora,* a small shrub from Brazil, which, in spite of its name, bears a surprising number of tubular-shaped flowers, bright orange at the base, shading to yellow at the tip; and *Coleus thyrsoideus,* a species from Central Africa which has spikes of bright blue flowers, also attracts attention.

Cestrum aurantiacum, with branched sprays of pale orange flowers, and Daturas do well, continuing to produce their huge scented flowers into winter.

The *Citrus* family is represented here by *Citrus medica,* the citron, with huge fruits used in the Jewish feast of the Tabernacles, a harvest festival. Citrons have been cultivated and used by the Jews since Roman times and are thought to have been found by them growing in Babylon, and brought back on their return from captivity. The thick rind provides the candied peel used for culinary purposes; *Citrus aurantium,* the Bitter Orange (this plant was presented to the Society by Yvonne Arnaud, the actress, after whom the theatre in nearby Guildford is named); and the small pot-plant + *Citrofortunella,* a chimera, or graft hybrid, with variegated foliage, which is covered in winter with miniature oranges.

Ornamental pot plants and house plants are displayed on staging around the edges of the temperate house, providing a colourful display, and are a means by which visitors can see for themselves the wide variety of forms available. *Cyclamen* hybrids and a range of Poinsettias (*Euphorbia pulcherrima*) are always of interest here, and less common but easily grown plants, such as *Aeschynanthus* 'Rubens', with striking orange flowers, can also be seen.

Despite the fact that we have mentioned a number of individual plants, it must be realised that this (and the adjacent two sections) is a *display* house, and that many of the plants are grown in one of the other houses and moved here when they are at their peak;

it also follows that exactly the same plants will not be seen every year – we have merely drawn attention to some that we consider to be of particular interest. Passing from the central to the cooler section, the visitor enters an area whose minimum temperature is in the region of 5°C, in other words, just providing protection from frosts and damp. This is likely to be of interest to the amateur gardener, who may baulk at keeping his greenhouse heated at 10°C, but might consider the lower temperature a good investment when he sees what can be grown in these conditions! For example *Acacia pravissima,* called the 'Ovens Wattle', an elegant small tree from south – eastern Australia, is covered with buds in January, and produces its rich yellow racemes of flowers during February and March under glass. It is hardy outdoors only in the mildest parts of Great Britain and Ireland, so for those who are not fortunate enough to live in such favoured parts, a greenhouse can help to enliven the winter! Another Australian wattle, the rather tender *Acacia baileyana,* also thrives here; it, too, flowers in early spring.

Other shrubs of interest in this section include *Dichroa febrifuga,* a relative of *Hydrangea,* whose shoots and bark are used against fever in the Himalaya around Darjeeling. Its pink buds open out into mauve flowers, and finally into berry-like fruits. The South African heath, *Erica canaliculata,* again hardy only in the milder parts of the country, makes a handsome bush about three metres high here, although in the wild it eventually attains a height of about twice that. The white, pink-flushed flowers appear during January, and contrast nicely with the rather greyish-looking young shoots. Another African, *Euryops pectinatus,* has attractive feathery silver foliage, which contrasts well with the bright yellow daisy flowers. It makes a bush about 1.5 metres high, and although it requires greenhouse treatment in England, it is one of the most popular garden shrubs in California.

The third section of the display house

The passion flower Passiflora coccinea, *almost perpetually in flower in the warm section of the display glasshouse.*

Next door to this house is another, even smaller greenhouse; here a range of conservatory shrubs, such as the pretty *Salvia leucantha*, which flowers in January, are kept frost-free. Outside in the garden is *Daphne bholua* 'Jaqueline Postill', a small shrub about 60 cm high, which bears very fragrant, pale pink flowers in January.

Alpine Department

The smaller of the two alpine houses is normally the most colourful at this time of year; this is because it is a display house, with plants grown in pans elsewhere and brought into the house when they are at their best. In contrast, the larger landscaped house contains a permanent collection of plants; it tends to be rather dull in midwinter, although there are a few interesting plants to be seen in flower here, such as the pale pink *Ranunculus calandrinoides*, from the Atlas Mountains, white *Chrysanthemum hosmariense* from Morocco, and the bright blue *Lithodora zahnii* from Greece. In the smaller house can be seen pans full of cyclamen, daffodils such as *Narcissus asturiensis*, a tiny species from north-west Spain, tulips such as *T. kolpakowskiana*, with lemon yellow flowers, and *T.schrenkii*, which has red petals tipped with yellow. There are masses of crocuses, such as the many attractive varieties of *Crocus chrysanthus*, one of which – the aptly-named 'Ladykiller' – has flashy white and purple flowers. In the drystone wall nearest the rock garden can be seen the attractive little feathery-leaved *Corydalis cheilanthifolia* from China, which has flowers of the palest lemon-yellow.

From the alpine department one can descend to the Rock Garden, pausing on the way to admire a fine specimen of *Clematis cirrhosa*, which is normally in full flower in January, and climbs up an oak tree at the northern end of the 'Monocot' borders.

is kept rather warmer and wetter, and here can be seen a collection of epiphytes and bromeliads. Some of these are very exotic in appearance, such as the cup-shaped *Aechmea podantha*, whose green leaves have pink tips, while others are familiar to many people as house-plants – examples being *Peperomia* and *Dieffenbachia*. *Canna iridiflora* also thrives here, making a clump over three metres high, and bearing large bright reddish-pink flowers.

Model Gardens

A brief visit to the nearby Scented Garden, in which is the small greenhouse containing a collection of perpetual-flowering carnations, can be recommended at this time of year; although this house measures only four by three metres, it can hold as many as a hundred and sixty plants, each in a small pot, which provide flowers throughout the year. The heady scent is possibly the chief attraction of these flowers, but the colour range is also superb, ranging from white through pale pinks and reds to the very dark red, almost black, of a variety such as 'Marchioness of Salisbury'.

The Rock Garden

The peat banks at the western end of the Rock Garden are the home of some very unusual hellebores. *Helleborus dumetorum* with rather small flowers,

has formed graceful hybrids with *H.orientalis*, and a green-flowered species, probably *H.cyclophyllus*, has formed a group of pure green-flowered hybrids.

In the bog garden at the foot of the Rock Garden a fine group of the purple-leaved *Bergenia purpurascens*, a species from the Himalaya, is conspicuous for the rich red colour of its leaves in winter, but it does also bear attractive pink flowers in spring. On the south-facing bank of the mound between the bog garden and the Wild Garden are many different garden varieties of *Pernettya mucronata*; these bear attractive large berries, in a wide range of colours, which remain on the plant from autumn through winter to the following spring.

The Bamboo Walk
The Bamboo Walk, which leads from Weather Hill Cottage to the corner of the Walled Garden, is another feature which is at its best in winter. The canes are

Colin Martin (see page 96) inspects a crop of winter lettuce in the Model Vegetable Garden.

Clematis cirrhosa on an old oak trunk at the top of the Rock Garden.

51

The fruits of Malus x robusta, *the Siberian crab apple, brighten a winter day in the Jubilee Arboretum.*

arched over by the weight of the wet leaves, forming a natural tunnel in rainy weather.

There are two species of the Chilean genus *Chusquea*, the commoner, taller *C.couleou*, and the dwarfer and rarer *C.breviglumis*. Bamboos tend to die after flowering, the same species flowering in different parts of the country simultaneously, usually over a period of a few years. The mechanism for this gregarious flowering is still not understood. At present flowers can be seen on the common bamboo *Pseudosasa japonica*, and the resultant weakening of the clumps, which used to have numerous stems up to 3 m tall, is very obvious. Other species which have still not flowered are in their full beauty, notably the delicate *Arundinaria nitida*, and *Phyllostachys flexuosa*, with wavy stems. Many more good bamboos can be seen in other areas of the Garden.

The Wild Garden

One of the chief joys of the Wild Garden in winter and early spring is the collection of witch hazels – *Hamamelis* species. The common name of these beautiful shrubs derives from the fact that the branches were used for water divining by the early settlers in New England as substitutes for hazel, and the bark was found to have medicinal uses. They thrive in the kind of soil to be found in this area of the Garden – that is, acid, moisture-retentive loam, with a helping of leafmould for good measure. There are six species, and several cultivars of *Hamamelis*, all of which make hardy, deciduous small trees or shrubs; spidery flowers, with four strap-shaped petals, are borne on the leafless branches, and are thus shown off to full advantage. Robert de Belder, a Belgian Vice President of the Society, and an authority on trees and shrubs, has selected a number of fine hybrids at his arboretum at Kalmthout, and several of these, such as *H*. x *intermedia* 'Jelena', named after his wife, and 'Diane' after his daughter, are to be seen in the Wild Garden. 'Jelena' has bright red and yellow flowers, which give a coppery appearance from a distance, and was given the Award of Merit in 1955. 'Ruby Glow' originally raised at Kalmthout by De Belder's predecessor, a Belgian nurseryman named Kort, can also be seen here, as can 'Magic Fire' ('Feuerzauber') which also has coppery-red flowers. All these x *intermedia*

Hamamelis mollis, *the Chinese witch-hazel, is one of many of the genus which flourishes in the Wild Garden.*

cultivars are hybrids of *H.mollis* and *H.japonica*.

H.mollis is probably the best known and finest of the witch hazels, and is a native of western and western central China. In a good season it will be covered with sweetly-scented golden-yellow blooms from December until March – and was awarded a First Class Certificate in 1918. There are a number of clones available, of which three, 'Pallida', 'Brevipetala' and 'Coombe Wood', are represented in the Wild Garden; two fine large specimens of the species can also be seen, covered in flowers, near to the Heather Garden. 'Pallida' is particularly beautiful, with lovely delicately-scented, pale yellow flowers in January and February, and was raised at Wisley from seeds that came either from Holland or Belgium (possibly Kalmthout again); some idea of its worth can be seen from the fact that it received an Award of Merit in 1932, a First Class Certificate in 1958 and the Award of Garden Merit in 1960. 'Coombe Wood', an old form with a rather spreading habit, has sweetly-scented, golden-yellow flowers. Another old variety is *H.japonica* 'Superba', with distinctly greeny-yellow flowers. Some of these cultivars are newly-planted, but many date from before the 1930's and have made fine specimens. Two other winter-flowering shrubs growing in this area deserve special mention- *Lonicera* x *purpusii* and *Viburnum* x *bodnantense* 'Dawn'. The first of these, a shrubby honeysuckle, bears its small white flowers in January and February, and is remarkable for the almost overwhelming sweet scent it produces; *Viburnum* 'Dawn' is also very fragrant, with attractive flowers which are rose-red when in bud, fading into a pinky-white after opening. 'Dawn' has an exceptionally long flowering season – usually from late autumn right through to early spring – and it is noticeable that the flower heads produced in spring are much larger and deeper pink than those borne in autumn and winter; it, and all the other x *bodnantense* hybrids, also have a link with the Society as they were raised at Bodnant in Wales, the home of the second and third Lords Aberconway, both President of the Society for many years (see also page 26).

As winter merges into spring the early rhododendrons and camellias come into flower; generally, by mid-February, the

Lenten roses,
Helleborus
orientalis, *in the Wild*
Garden, in February.

following, on the northern side of this area, are in full flower: a neat little bush of *Rhododendron keiskei,* which has small greeny-yellow flowers, and two good camellias – C. 'Marguerite Gouillon', with small double flowers, pale pink with darker pink stripes, and C. 'C.M.Hovey', which has large deep pink flowers. In the central part of the Wild Garden are many different *Pieris,* one of which, aptly named 'Flamingo', has flowers which are bright pink rather than the usual white, and dozens of different kinds of hellebores, whose flowers vary in colour from the bright green of *H.lividus* to the very dark blackish- red of *H.* 'Pluto'. On the south-facing edge of this area are two fine tall specimens of *Rhododendron calophytum,* a species from western China; they are around ten metres high, and covered with large trusses of pale pink flowers. In addition to trees and shrubs, this area contains many fine bulbs and herb-aceous plants – as it did in G.F. Wilson's

time (see page 16). There are carpets of the little *Narcissus cyclamineus* and a lovely group of *N.* 'Dove Wings', which has a golden-yellow trumpet and pale yellow reflexed petals. Those with sharp eyes might be able to spot the mouseplant, *Arisarum proboscoideum,* whose flowers have a long extension to the spathe which looks like the tail of a mouse, sticking up out of the leaves. A pretty little primrose, *Primula vulgaris* 'Gigha White', thrives here as do both pink and blue pulmonarias.

From here it is worth making a short diversion to the south-facing outside wall of the walled formal gardens where a number of precocious bulbs and climbers enjoy the warmth and shelter. The elegant evergreen *Clematis cirrhosa* is one such, producing its modest scented pale yellow flowers throughout the winter and early spring; its attractive fern-like leaves become bronze-coloured in winter, providing the perfect foil for the flowers. Nearby, is

the closely-related *C. napaulensis*, of rather doubtful hardiness, as can be seen in the fact that it was given an Award of Merit in 1957 as a plant for the cool greenhouse; however, such is its beauty that it is well worth trying in warm situations in the milder counties. The flowers, which, like those of *C.cirrhosa* are cup-shaped, but even better scented, are creamy yellow, with contrasting purple stamens and anthers, and are borne on young growths throughout the winter.

In the bed at the foot of this same wall are two attractive irises – *I. unguicularis* (formerly known to everyone as *I.stylosa*) 'Mary Barnard' and *Iris lazica*. *I unguicularis* comes from Algeria and Greece and so is used to warm winter weather. Its glaucous foliage is evergreen, and makes an attractive background to the flowers, which are lilac-coloured, and normally borne from about October to March, depending on the weather of the previous summer.

'Mary Barnard' is an excellent dark-coloured form; *Iris lazica* is similar, but has broader green leaves.

Seven Acres

Seven Acres contains many shrubs and trees of interest in winter; here can be seen good flowering specimens of *Viburnum* x *bodnantense*, *Chaenomeles japonica* var. *alpina*, with bright pink flowers in late winter, and *Chaenomeles* x *californica* 'California' Elsewhere in Seven Acres *Prunus subhirtella* 'Autumnalis' and *Hamamelis macrophylla* will be in full flower in December, while *Osmanthus delavayii* produces its clusters of small, sweet-smelling white flowers towards the beginning of spring. There is a good collection of *Berberis* species and hybrids in Seven Acres, amongst them *B.* 'Barbarossa', *B.darwinii*, *B.replicata*, *B.* 'Bunch o' Grapes' and *B.* 'Autumn Beauty'; the species have attractive flowers, while 'Bunch o' Grapes' is, as

Narcissus cyclamineus in the Wild Garden.

Seven Acres under snow.

The Round Pond on a good skating day!

the name suggests, covered with small bunches of berries, and 'Autumn Beauty' has striking orange foliage.

Towards the end of February, visitors walking by the Round Pond are rewarded by the sight of a colony of the diminutive *Narcissus cyclamineus* growing at the water's edge.

The Heather Garden

Some heathers continue to give a good display of colour, either from their flowers or foliage, through the winter and into the spring; two of particular note are *Eric carnea* and *E.x darleyensis,* the hybrid between *E.carnea* and the Irish native *E.erigena.* By the New Year the large tree heathers begin to come into bud; the first to flower is *E.lusitanica,* from Portugal, closely followed by *E.x veitchii,* its hybrid with *E.arborea,* which at Wisley makes a large shrub up to nearly three metres high. *E.arborea* itself flowers in early spring, and it, and its variety 'Alpina', make a very striking bush. A large clump of a form of the common ling, *Calluna vulgaris* 'Oxshott Common', is attractive also, having grey hairy foliage – an adaptation to the poor dry sandy soil of its native heathland.

Pinetum

The Pinetum is situated to the north of Seven Acres, and is separated from Howards Field by a small wood of Scots Pine which G.F. Wilson had planted in about 1898. The first conifers were planted in the pinetum in 1908, and in 1927 a broad walk was made right through it, crossing the public footpath by a bridge. The severe storm of October 1987 caused much damage in this area, although fortunately many of the most impressive specimens escaped unhurt. In tandem with the cleaning-up operations, a number of new features are planned for this area, including the planting of evergreen azaleas and flowering cherries to provide spring colour, and the addition of Japanese maples, *Cornus* and *Hamamelis* to provide interest in the autumn.

Amongst the many fine specimens of trees still to be seen in the Pinetum are a very large *Cupressus glabra* (over 20 metres high), x *Cupressocyparis leylandii* (about 28 metres high), two fine specimens of *Pinus holfordiana, Picea breweriana, Pinus radiata,* and *Pseudotsuga menziesii* 'Fretsii'. Returning to the laboratory by way of the formal pool one sees a small group of the pretty little double-headed *Narcissus* 'Tête-à-Tête', and, against the lab wall, a fine large specimen of *Camellia japonica* 'Princess Charlotte', an old variety which has the strange habit of bearing pink, white, and bicoloured flowers.

A stand of pines between Howards Field and the Pinetum; many of these were felled in the great storm.

The enlarged restaurant , opened in the autumn of 1988. The tower, described by the architects as 'jettied mediaeval', is intended to link the new building with the style of the Laboratory; the best place to get a good view of both is from the top of Battleston Hill.

The Work of the Laboratory

The laboratory building, which many visitors assume to be old, was in fact built only in 1914-16; further details of its construction may be found on page 23. It houses both the offices of the Director, the Curator, and the administrative staff, and the laboratory where the Society's staff provide advisory services for members and conduct scientific research connected with horticulture.

General advisory work

Questions relating to horticulture in general, on cultivation of plants and especially lawns, weed control, availability of plants and gardening aids are answered by the Horticultural Advisor, Mr David Pycraft, who first came to Wisley as a student in 1960. Mr Pycraft was later a member of the 1963 Bowles Scholarship Botanical Expedition to Iran and Turkey (see illustration on page 35) and joined the staff of the Society in 1964. His knowledge is vast and is backed up by his own continually revised data files; the queries he receives are sometimes in the national interest (for example, which would be the most hardwearing type of grass suitable for use at Stonehenge), sometimes of the utmost importance to the questioner (as in the case of the Arab who arrived complete with an entourage of bodyguards and demanded to know the most effective type of anti-terrorist hedge), and sometimes just plain silly (such as the lady who wanted to know how she could prevent her cats from drowning in her neighbour's new garden pool). Nearly three thousand enquiries, usually perfectly sensible!, are dealt with each year.

The School of Horticulture

The influence of Wisley on horticulture has been spread throughout the world, mainly by those horticulturists who trained at the Garden. The Society, almost from its earliest days, had regarded the training of young men as gardeners as a high priority, and in the *Transactions of the Horticultural Society of London*, published in 1820, it stated that the Society "*Looked forward with confidence to that period when .... they may effect an establishment, which shall .... become a National School for the propagation of Horticultural knowledge ....*". The Society subsequently began a two-year training programme in its garden at Chiswick, whereby the students were paid a wage in return for working in the garden, were provided with a small library, and were found jobs on completion of their training; the most famous student of this era was Joseph Paxton, designer of the Crystal Palace.

Shortly after moving to Wisley, a new course was set up, using the small laboratory as headquarters; the students paid an admission fee of five guineas, receiving in exchange lectures, instruction and practical work in the garden. Courses similar to this have been continued until the present day, with students (who are now paid) working in the garden learning practical skills from the senior garden staff. The students also have evening lectures after work on topics such as fungicides and pesticides, plant pathology and

A birch tree with striking white bark, Betula 'Grayswood Ghost', can be seen at the southern end of Seven Acres.

entomology. The wide range of rare plants grown at Wisley is one of the garden's specialities, and the students are given identification tests of plants flowering in the garden every fortnight. The opportunity thus afforded has meant that plant knowledge has also always been one of the special strengths of Wisley-trained horticulturists, standing them in good stead in their subsequent employment in Britain or abroad.

Over the years a large number of foreign students have enrolled on the Wisley course, and in 1987 the first student from China arrived from the Kunming Institute of Botany. Several of the British students have taken up posts abroad, and these contacts help the horticultural 'old-boy' network throughout the world, and English ex-Wisley students are now working in North America, the West Indies, France, Belgium, and so on.

The Wisley student course has recently been changed, and is now designed to meet the needs of older students, both male and female, who have already completed degree courses elsewhere. This is a return to the system which was in operation until 1972; from 1972 to 1988/9, the majority of students were school leavers on a two-year course, although several short-term students were also taken on each year for periods of six months to a year. It has been found that the older students, in general, are more motivated and gain more from the course than did the younger school leavers.

Botany

The botany department is concerned mainly with the naming of garden plants. Specimens sent or brought into the laboratory by members of the Society will be named: they may be old roses or other plants found in an overgrown garden, or bits and pieces brought back from foreign holidays. Very few plants cannot be named provided the specimen is adequate.

The botany department also has the difficult task of overseeing the labelling of plants in the Garden: for checking the labels of new plants, and making sure that the existing plants in the Garden are wearing their correct labels – not an easy task when visitors take a liking to a particular plant and put the label in their pocket so that they can remember the name when they get home. Lists of new plants are sent in to the department by the superintendents of each area, and are checked before being passed on to the label department where the label is cut.

Wisley is one of the few gardens which keeps an herbarium of cultivated plants – that is, a collection of dried pressed specimens labelled with their name and place of origin. This is very useful for checking plant names, both of wild species and especially of cultivars. Unlike the wild species which have to be properly described in Latin when they are first named, garden cultivars have no published descriptions by which they may be checked, so they are much harder to identify accurately.

The Curator's office is now responsible for the Entry Book in which all the new plants or seeds coming in to the Garden are listed, with their origins. This makes fascinating, but at the same time, frustrating, reading; to know how many exciting plants have come and gone, compared with how few have succeeded and remained as permanent residents of gardens. Many which came from parts of the world now inaccessible, for instance, from Afghanistan or Iran, abode a year or two, then went their way.

Members of the botany department, in common with other members of the Wisley scientific staff, act as secretaries to the various committees which meet at the Flower Shows in London (including Chelsea Show) to judge plants, and so they get to know the members of the committees, many of whom are specialists in their particular field, and thus able to shed light on obscure plants. This contact with august members of the Society could be regarded as one of the advantages of being a committee secretary. John Elsley, botanist to the Society in the 1960's, had reason to be thankful for it. He

Winter Aconites brighten one of the terrace beds by the Laboratory, before the leaves of hostas emerge in late spring.

supplemented his salary by making use of tips provided by Lord Blakenham, then the Society's Treasurer, Chairman of Floral Committee 'B' and a noted racehorse owner. One horse, Boxer, was entered for the Cheltenham Spring Meeting, and the odds offered the previous autumn were thirty to one. John Elsley acted promptly on this recommendation, staking the then not inconsiderable sum of £10, and the horse duly won the Daily Express Triumph Hurdle, starting favourite, enabling the botanist to buy his first car. The members of the botany department also conduct taxonomic research into garden plants. Peter Barnes, the present Botanist, who has been at Wisley since 1974, is an expert on ferns, hebes and several other genera. He and the other members of the Botany Department, Diana Miller and Adrian Whiteley, contribute accounts of particular genera to the *European Garden Flora* and the new *RHS Dictionary of Plants*.

Entomology

Questions concerning garden pests, such as slugs, aphids, red spider mite or caterpillars, are answered by the entomology department. The entomologist, Andrew Halstead, has been at Wisley since 1972, and in this time has seen and dealt with every pest the gardener is likely to encounter. In addition to dealing with members queries, records are kept of moths caught in a mercury vapour light trap which is lit in the Garden every night as part of the Rothamsted Insect Survey. It is perhaps surprising that, in spite of the well-publicised increase in the use of pesticides and in the intensity of farming, the numbers of moths have remained more or less constant. About three hundred species are recorded every year, and an insect collection is kept in the department.

Plant Registration

Parallel to the work of the botany department is that of Plant Registration. The Society acts as the International Registration Authority for several genera including conifers, dahlias, delphiniums, *Dianthus*, lilies, *Narcissus*, orchids and rhododendrons. All new cultivars of these groups named anywhere in the world should be registered with the Registration Officer at Wisley, Dr Alan Leslie, whose work includes compiling, publishing and maintaining registers of all known cultivar names within each group. The point of this system is to attempt to ensure that each cultivar name is used only once within each group, thus avoiding confusion to both commercial growers and amateur gardeners. The Society is much involved with this work, the Chairman of the International Commission for Nomenclature and Registration, which oversees all registration, being the Director General of the Society, Mr C.D. Brickell.

Dr Leslie is well-known in England on account of his extensive knowledge of the Surrey flora, and he has recently privately published a *Supplement and Checklist* to the *Flora of Surrey*, by J.E. Lousley (1976). He has also, with Mr Brickell, undertaken a trip to China as a guest of the Kunming Institute of Botany.

As part of its work with the standardisation of plant names and descriptions, the RHS published, in 1966, a Colour Chart. It was reprinted in 1984 in association with the Flower Council of Holland. It includes eight hundred numbered colours, enabling people (and not just gardeners, as we shall see) to check colours against a written description. Many enquiries concerning the chart are received from callers as varied as dairies (for the colouring agents used in yoghurt), textile and paint manufacturers, and, by far the most unusual, an Irishman from County Monaghan, who rang from the police station (an officer or an inmate?) and spoke to David Pycraft, wanting information on the Colour Chart as he felt it would be indispensible to his fly-tying!

Plant Pathology
The Plant Pathology department answers questions on all kinds of plant diseases and disorders, chiefly those caused by funguses of one type or another. The staff are faced with specimens of dead and dying plants and have to identify the cause of death or disease, or try to isolate possible pathogens.

Miss Audrey Brooks, who has been pathologist since 1964, is Wisley's Senior Scientist, a position carrying with it such tasks as the devising and overseeing of the students course, and responsibility for much of the overall work of the Laboratory. Her assistant is Miss Pippa Greenwood, who has worked at Wisley since 1985; her particular interest is in Honey Fungus. Over two thousand five hundred enquiries are answered by the Pathology department each year: most are familiar, but some new diseases appear, or become commoner each year – notes on such phenomena have been published in *The Garden*. New diseases noted recently include Chrysanthemum White Rust, which is now unfortunately common on amateur's chrysanthemums; Hypericum Rust, which has spread from its usual host H. 'Elstead' onto other species, including the Rose of Sharon, *H.calycinum*; and Cupressus Canker, which causes die-back of cypresses and x *Cupressocyparis,* sometimes killing the bark around the trunk and causing the sudden death of the tree.

Photography
The Society has, over the years, built up a good collection of photographs, some of which, such as the early lantern slides reproduced at the beginning of this book (page 25) are now of historical interest. Mr Bob Scase, for many years Librarian at Wisley, maintained and added to the collection, and sets of slides for use in lectures to local horticultural societies affiliated to the RHS, were and still are, available for hire from the Publicity Officer at Wisley. The present photographer at Wisley is Mr Wilf Halliday, who is a Fellow of the Royal Photographic Society; the majority of the colour photographs in this book were taken by him.

Painting
Unlike the great Botanic Gardens, such as Kew, Wisley does not have a tradition

of having botanical or horticultural artists on the staff; the one exception to this (as far as we have been able to discover) being the employment for a number of years of Mr A.J. Wise, an artist of considerable talent. A large collection of his paintings are stored at Wisley, amongst them many fine studies of irises (see illustration right), and these have recently been catalogued by Mrs Miller (see page 61). It seems that Mr Wise and Frank Knight (Director of the Garden at the time) enjoyed what might be described as a stormy relationship – Wise would come into work later and later each day, looking more and more disreputable, until Mr Knight could stand it no more and would sack him. The next day Wise would appear promptly at nine o'clock in his best suit, and carry on working as usual. According to David Pycraft, who is one of the few members of staff to remember him, this happened quite regularly; whatever his failings might have been, A.J. Wise left behind him a quantity of fine paintings, and it is to be hoped that they will one day be exhibited to the public.

Director and Curator

Last, but certainly not least, we mention the men who currently hold these two important, and interdependent, posts: Philip McMillan Browse and Jim Gardiner. Mr McMillan Browse graduated with a B.Sc. in Horticulture from the University of Nottingham, and was subsequently Head of the Department of Horticulture at Brooksby Agricultural College in Leicestershire, and Senior Lecturer in Nursery Practices at Hadlow College of Agriculture and Horticulture in Kent, before becoming Director of the Saratoga Horticultural Foundation in San Martin, California. While in California, Mr McMillan Browse searched for good forms of native plants, and introduced a number of them into cultivation. He is particularly interested in the propagation of woody plants, and also hopes to encourage the cultivation of a number of plants of Californian origin at Wisley.

Iris 'Romance', A.M. after trial at Wisley in 1931, painted in 1933 by A.J. Wise.

Mr Jim Gardiner joined the Wisley staff in March 1988, having previously been Curator first of the Liverpool City Botanic Gardens and then of the well-known Hillier Arboretum in Hampshire. Together, Mr Gardiner and Mr McMillan Browse have drawn up an ambitious plan for the restructuring of the Garden, an extract from which is quoted on page 43; this is partly in response to the devastation caused by the great storm in 1987, and partly because some areas of the Garden are over-visited, while other parts are under-used. Possibly for the first time in its history, major changes are to be carried out at Wisley, imposing a design on what has previously been a garden that 'just growed': surely, this must be a good thing, and it is to be hoped that members and employees of the Society will continue to feel proud of their garden.

Spring

SPRING is probably the most exciting season for any gardener, the time when bare branches give way to acid green leaves, the first bulbs push up through the grass, and camellias, rhododendrons and azaleas are covered with buds. All these things, and many more, can be seen at Wisley between March and May, and this is always a rewarding time of year to visit the garden. In the following pages we describe some areas which are at their most interesting at this time, but of course there are many fascinating plants and trees dotted about in other parts of the garden which are also good in spring – we just do not have enough room to describe them all here.

Many people particularly appreciate the 'wild' areas, where plants are displayed in a natural way, as in the Wild Garden and the Alpine Meadow. The Wild Garden is the oldest part of the garden at Wisley, having been originally planted by Mr G.F. Wilson during the 1880's (see page 16). Adjacent is the Alpine Meadow, where drifts of the little hoop-petticoat narcissus and other small bulbs flow over a grassy slope, broken by rocky outcrops.

Some people like to see more exotic plants in a simulated natural setting – and this taste should be amply satisfied by a visit to Battleston Hill. Here an enormous collection of camellias, rhododendrons and azaleas is to be seen, although the great storm of October 1987 has removed many of the mature trees from the hill.

On those days when the English spring seems more akin to an arctic winter, a visit to the green-houses is recommended; here one can stroll amongst orchids, see the huge flowers of *Camellia reticulata* protected from the weather, gaze on an Arizonan desert or wander along paths overhung with lush scented semi-tropical vegetation – a heart and hand-warming experience.

Primula pulverulenta, globe flowers (Trollius), evergreen azaleas and a large pink rhododendron, seen here at the edge of the Wild Garden, looking out to the corner of the Alpine Meadow.

A view towards the main entrance of the garden; in the foreground is Clematis montana *'Tetrarose', climbing up the corner of the Laboratory.*

On entering the garden, visitors pass through a pair of wrought-iron gates commemorating the Rev. W. Wilks, one time Secretary of the Society and an able gardener. The poppies depicted in the design represent the Shirley poppies, a strain which Wilks raised from the seed of a single unusual-coloured plant of the wild corn poppy, *Papaver rhoeas*. In addition to his work as Secretary of the Society, Wilks was vicar of Shirley, Croydon, where he created an interesting garden; it is after this place that the poppies were named.

Once inside the gates, the visitor passes on the left the Garden House, built for the first Garden Superintendent, S.T. Wright (see page 20) and the south wall of the Laboratory on the right. Keeping straight on, up a narrow flight of steps, the path leads to the main terrace, a grassy rectangle enclosed by hornbeam hedges. The circular beds set in the lawn are filled with appropriate bedding plants, chosen to give a bright display throughout the season; in spring tulips, forget-me-nots, pansies or polyanthus are often used, and these are followed by sun-loving plants such as African daisies of various types, or sometimes *Impatiens*. Running south from this terrace is the Broadwalk, which, as the name implies, is a wide grassy walk leading between two long, mainly herbaceous, borders up to Battleston Hill.

Battleston Hill

Battleston Hill is the east-west ridge of high ground which runs from the glasshouse area across the top of the Broad Walk and ends close to the A3 road near the turning to Wisley. It is bisected by a public footpath which by law cannot be blocked or diverted, so has to be fenced to prevent unauthorised visitors entering the garden. Those already inside the garden can cross the footpath by a wooden footbridge on the crest of the hill, and there is a second bridge at the bottom of the south side of the hill, by the Trials field.

The crest of Battleston Hill took the full force of the 1987 storm, and was utterly changed, with many fine and ancient oaks blown down or so damaged that they had to be removed (see photograph on p.43). One particularly sad loss on the near side of the footpath was a large tree of *Eucalyptus dalrympleana*, planted in 1959, with beautiful white and grey bark, peeling in sheets; it had survived many cold winters and lesser storms unharmed. Another loss which had great visual impact on the garden was the fine oak which stood in the middle of the Broadwalk, near the crest of the hill, forming a focal point for the vista up the borders from near the entrance, and a cool viewpoint from which to look over a wide sweep of the garden. However, this 'thinning' of the tree cover has led to increased opportunities for development of the area, and a number of new planting schemes are being considered.

One new development is to be seen on the south-facing bank of the hill, which has been cleared and terraced with old railway sleepers, to provide a home for sun-loving shrubs from Australia, California and the Mediterranean area. At the time of writing, this work is still under way, so no full description of the plants to be seen in this area can be given.

The north-facing area at the top of the Broadwalk remains spectacular, with large numbers of rhododendrons, camellias, azaleas and magnolias and other woody plants. Many of these were originally planted as trials of new rhododendron and azalea cultivars, and the best have been allowed to remain and become mature, to act as a yardstick for modern varieties. One of the newer trials is that of *Rhododendron yakushimanum* hybrids. *R.yakushimanum* grows high up on the small, subtropical island of Yakushima, off the south coast of Japan; in its wild state – due to the altitude at which it grows – *R.yakushimanum* enjoys wet, misty conditions, on rocky bluffs and around the edges of bogs, very different to the dry, sandy soil on Battleston Hill. It is, in its best forms, an exceptionally compact and slow growing plant, free-flowering and hardy. The aim of the hybrids is to

Part of the trial of evergreen azaleas on Battleston Hill.

Hosta' Undulata', a small hybrid grown chiefly for its foliage, although it also bears rich lilac – coloured flowers in early summer. There is a large collection of hostas on Battleston Hill.

retain the low-growing, compact habit, and introduce different flower colours, making an ideal shrub for planting in small gardens. Here on Battleston Hill, however, some specimens (many of which were planted in 1973) have become more drawn up than is usual; whether the loss of tree cover will make any difference to this or not remains to be seen. In the meantime the trials of these, and other plants, enable visitors to judge for themselves the eventual appearance of, and amount of space required for, a wide choice of different varieties.

Most rhododendrons and evergreen

Primula bhutanica
needs a very cool and
shady position, and
thrives on the north
side of Battleston Hill.

interest and beauty in the 1960's. Originally it was a pine plantation, with some large old oaks, and was thus ideal for Himalayan shrubs, camellias and other plants which prefer acid soil and need some shelter and shade in summer. The path along the crest of the hill is known as the Burma road.

On the north-facing side of the hill, shrubs which require cooler, moister conditions were planted; many made fine specimens, including a large specimen of the single white *Camellia* 'Francis Hanger', a x *williamsii* hybrid of great refinement. There were many rare rhododendrons, both species and hybrids such as 'General Sir John du Cane' which made a small tree, often covered with large scented pink waxy flowers. A spreading shrub of *Prunus mume* 'Beni-shi-Dori' was exciting in early spring, with red, scented flowers on slender green twigs. Also early-flowering were large shrubs of *Hamamelis mollis* and the rare and tender cherry, *Prunus campanulata,* with small, deep pink flowers on long stalks. At the foot of the hill, in one of the coolest spots in the whole garden, were a series of peat banks planted with dwarf alpine rhododendrons, cassiopes, gentians and *Meconopsis,* and a fine display of the ice-blue *Primula bhutanica* which flowers in February and March. This lovely primrose is not difficult to grow even in the south of England, provided that hot summer sun never falls onto the leaves. It will grow happily even in complete shade, as long as it is kept cool and moist in summer.

The southern side of Battleston Hill also contained a fine collection of rhododendrons. Different forms of *Rhododendron* x *loderi,* including the creamy-yellow 'Milkmaid', were planted along a diagonal path. Nearby, in complete contrast, were the small tubular orange bells of *R. keysii,* a rare species from Bhutan and Tibet. Magnolias were a feature of this area, and there were good specimens of the Japanese *M. hypoleuca,* with upright scented flowers and large leaves. *Paulownia fargesii,* the western Chinese equivalent of the commoner eastern

and hybrid azaleas are at their best during May – with the later-flowering ones continuing until mid-June. During the early spring, however, there is still plenty to be seen, with groups of many varieties of daffodils edging the paths, and the young leaves of hostas emerging. Most of the camellias, large numbers of which are planted on the east side of Battleston Hill, are also at their best during March and April.

The part of the hill across the bridge on the far side of the public footpath was even more severely damaged, and a year later had still not been reopened to visitors. It probably reached its peak of

Chinese *P. tomentosa*, had made a large tree and often flowered well, although it was planted too high on the slope for its flowers to be seen at their best.

The upper part of the south slope is interrupted by an enclosed dell, whose steep banks are much used by badgers for a sett. This area could be viewed from the Burma road, and contained hardy palms (*Trachycarpus fortunei*) and large-leaved rhododendrons such as *R. falconeri*, which however find the climate of Wisley too dry for optimal growth. One striking specimen here was *Rhododendron* 'Calarbor', a hybrid between *R. calophytum* and *R. arboreum*, which had made a sturdy tree, and was exceptionally free-flowering with white claret-blotched flowers in large, compact trusses.

The western end of the slope contained the trial of *Camellia* x *williamsii* cultivars, as well as several old specimens of *C. saluenensis*, their other parent with *C. japonica*. It could be recognised by its small flowers of a rather purplish-pink, and finely toothed, not shining leaves. This trial was a fine sight when in flower. The best known of these hybrids is 'Donation', and it was interesting to compare it with other hybrids of similar parentage, including the small-flowered single 'J.C. Williams', and the very large 'Brigadoon'.

The sunny side of the hill also proved suitable for growing many bulbs which preferred a warm site, and provided colour in late summer after the shrubs had mostly finished. Large groups of lilies such as the Bellingham hybrids bred in America and the coloured trumpet lilies from Oregon Bulb Farms were often a fine sight, and groups of the first *L.lankongense* hybrids raised by Chris North at Mylnefield, near Dundee, grew well. The climate, soil and aspect proved ideal for hardy *Agapanthus*, and large clumps lined many of the paths. There was a trial of *Agapanthus*, held in around 1973, so that Wisley has an especially good collection of hardy species and cultivars.

At the bottom of this area was a large planting of rhododendrons, many of

Rhododendron 'Calarbor' forms a very large shrub or small tree, and flowers in the early spring. Seen here growing on Battleston Hill – there is also one in the Wild Garden.

Camellia x williamsii 'Anticipation'; a trial of C.x williamsii cultivars can be seen on Battleston Hill.

which were unnamed seedlings raised by Francis Hanger (p.31). Hundreds must have been planted out, and hundreds more lost or for some reason abandoned, because, over ten years later, when searching for a label beneath some beautifully-flowering hybrid, I came across a box of hundreds of zinc labels, buried in the mulch; all were ready for putting out on young plants, hand-written with a code number etched with fluoric acid. How long they had been there, or how they came to be hidden, I have never discovered. Many of Hanger's rhododendrons received awards, others were almost as beautiful, but never named or propagated.

By the early 1980's many of the pine trees were becoming dangerous through age and had to be felled. This caused some areas to become too open and dry, and although new trees were planted, they have not had time to become established and provide much-needed shade.

Plans for future development aim to exploit to the full the natural features of the land, and to introduce more varied planting. It may be possible to introduce water on top of the ridge, a naturally dry area, and have a stream draining into a reflecting pool in the bottom of the dell. The north slope will again house a collection of rhododendrons, camellias and magnolias; the south slope will concentrate on deciduous trees and shrubs, selected for their autumn colour and tolerance of a hot, dry, site.

Portsmouth Field

Turning south from Battleston Hill, the visitor comes to the Portsmouth Field – so called from its proximity to the old Portsmouth Road – which is where the majority of trials at Wisley are carried out. During early spring there is unlikely to be a great display of colour for the visitor, but there is nevertheless always plenty going on by way of pre-paration for the next years trials. By the beginning of March some of the plots (particularly those designated for vegetable trials) are being given the last touches with the rake prior to seed sowing, having been double-dug with manure in late autumn; by watching this, and other operations, the novice can pick up many handy tips to try out later at home! Some of the staff involved in trials work at Wisley have been here for many years, and to watch them at work is to enjoy a master-class of the highest order. Another way of learning from the RHS staff's experience is to watch an official Demonstration. These – and Garden Walks – are regularly arranged, details of dates and times being published in *The Garden*, Journal of the RHS, which is sent free to all members of the Society.

A great variety of vegetables (common and exotic) and other plants of all kinds are grown under trial at Wisley, and new types are being tested all the time. Within the last few years – to give a random selection – trials of antirrhin-ums, aubergines, broad beans, chrysan-themums, courgettes, daffodils, dahlias, Florence fennel, irises, leeks, parsley, pinks, pumpkins and squashes, sweet peas and sugar peas, have all been carried out, and the results published, so that the visitor can make an informed choice when selecting varieties for his or her garden.

At the eastern end of the trials field is an area shaded by large oak trees which were miraculously spared in the hurricane. This is known as the Winter Garden, and is fully described on page 46; as the name suggests, many of the plants there flower in winter, but there is much that remains into spring.

Alpine Department

Bulbous plants of all types are always of interest in the spring, and a good collection is to be seen in the alpine department which is situated to the south of the Rock Garden. In the larger greenhouse (made of aluminium and measuring 9 by 10 metres) plants are permanently grown in limestone and sandstone rock, covered with 'scree', and landscaped to give as natural an effect as possible. This 'covered rock garden' provides good growing conditions for many alpines, especially those from high altitudes which require protection from the dampness of the

John Warwick (formerly Superintendent of the Rock Garden) lays slabs of stone in the larger of the two new alpine houses.

English climate, and winter-flowering bulbs. Amongst the diversity of species to be seen here are *Androsace, Draba, Dionysia* and other 'cushion' plants; *Origanum* and *Lithodora,* which like warm conditions; and dwarf species of *Aquilegia, Campanula* and *Dicentra,* which enjoy the cool root-runs to be found in the rock crevices.

Some changes are being made within this house; the beds are to be raised up more, and sandstone will be used on the shadier side of the path, with limestone on the sunny side. Ventilation, shading and irrigation are also being altered, in an attempt to improve the conditions for those plants which cannot tolerate much heat and drought.

Among the bulbous plants to be seen during the spring are *Cyclamen* species, some of which are twenty or thirty years old!, and *Narcissus,* such as *N.romieuxii* (similar in appearance to *N.bulbocodium*), *N.watieri,* a rare dwarf white species from Morocco, and *N. cyclamineus. Tecophilaea cyanocrocus* 'Violacea' can also be seen in this house; the usual colour is a deep gentian blue, and there is also a var. *leichtlinii* with a white – throated flower. *Tecophilaea* is a beautiful small plant, a native of Chile, where it grows on stony slopes pro-

tected by snow in winter. The name, which means 'lover of children', is derived from Tecophila, the daughter of an Italian lawyer, L.A.Colla (1866-1848) who described plants collected by M.D. Bertero in the 1830's. Since then, it is feared that the plant has become extinct in the wild, due to over-grazing and over-enthusiastic collecting, although fortunately there are many plants in cultivation in both public and private gardens, so that it may one day be possible to re-establish it in its native habitat.

Non-bulbous plants of interest include *Teucrium webbianum* from southeast Spain, *Ranunculus calandrinioides* and *Soldanella carpatica. Ranunculus calandrinioides* is a native of Morocco where it grows in the Middle Atlas, near cedar forests, producing pale pink flowers in March and April, though frequently in autumn or winter as well as spring in the alpine house. It is dormant in summer and survives drought with its tuberous roots. A smaller, but rather similar species, requires the same treatment; this is *R.acetosellifolius* which makes sheets of the palest pink flowers near the melting snow on the high plateau of the Sierra Nevada in southeastern Spain.

The smaller alpine house, showing pots of alpines plunged in gravel.

Bowles' Scholarship Expedition to Iran, Brickell & Mathew, Marr, Rix and more recently the Linzee-Gordons; a few are still growing even from P.H.Davis's expeditions to Turkey in the 1950's and those of E.K. Balls in the late thirties. As well as for their beauty, these collected bulbs were of clear scientific value when accounts of various bulbous genera were being written for *Flora Europaea*, the *Flora of Turkey*, and the *European Garden Flora*. Several of these were written by members of the Wisley scientific staff.

The alpine department has also been the source, or at least the point of distribution, of many special Wisley plants. Examples are *Ipheion uniflorum* 'Wisley Blue', *Saxifraga grisebachii* 'Wisley var.', and *Iris afghanica*, collected by the Furses, but increased at Wisley. *Tropaeolum tuberosum* 'Ken Aslet', a day-neutral and therefore summer-flowering variety of the edible-rooted climbing nasturtium of the Andes, is named after a former superintendent of the Rock Garden department; he recognised its value and gave it to Ken Beckett who propagated, distributed and named it. *Verbascum* 'Letitia', named after Ken Aslet's wife Letty, was a chance seedling, almost certainly a hybrid between *V. dumulosum* from the ruins of Termessos, and *V. spinosum* from Crete, both collected by Peter Davis and grown together in the Wisley alpine house.

Soldanella carpatica, a close relative of *S.alpina* which is so common in the Alps, is found in the western Carpathians in Czechoslovakia and Poland. It differs from *S.alpina* mainly in having stalked glands on the flowering stem, but it also has leaves which are often purple on the underside.

The smaller (12 by 4 metres) of the two houses is constructed of western red cedar and contains staging on which pans of alpines are displayed. Plants for this house, unlike the permanent planting in the landscaped house, are brought on in the alpine frameyard (not open to visitors) and displayed on the benches when they are at their peak. This method of cultivation is naturally more labour-intensive than the other, and it may be of interest to visitors to compare the two ways of growing and displaying plants.

This is where most of the spring-flowering bulbs will be seen, particularly dwarf *Narcissus*, irises, fritillaries and *Cyclamen*, all of which do well in pots. Many of them are still the same clones which were collected around twenty years ago by the Furse's expeditions, the

The area immediately surrounding the two houses described above is divided into three levels retained by dry stone walls. On the lowest level, at the north end of the site, stand a number of hypertufa sinks and stone troughs, planted with a variety of alpines; hypertufa is made up of equal parts of peat, cement and sand and can be stuck with strong glue to the surface of an old glazed sink or other suitable container. One of the obvious advantages of growing alpines in a trough or sink is that so little space is required; even in the smallest garden a corner can usually be found for a few choice plants. A Wisley Handbook, entitled *Alpines the Easy Way*, is published by the RHS and available from RHS Enterprises at Wisley and this gives sound advice to the amateur wishing to grow alpines.

One retaining wall, which is constructed of Sussex sandstone, houses specimens of *Ramonda* and *Haberlea*; at the base of this is a shady, north-facing bed, which contains a number of interesting plants, notably the hardy orchid *Dactylorhiza elata*, a native of the Mediterranean region, and *Sanguinaria canadensis* 'Flore Pleno', from North America.

The second drystone wall is constructed of Devon slate from a quarry near Tavistock, and has many plants, notably ferns, incorporated into the vertical surface – this planting is always best done at the construction stage, if possible. Particularly happy here are the Lewisias, which love well-drained conditions, and having their rosettes of fleshy leaves planted on their sides.

Adjacent to the smaller greenhouse is a south-facing wall built of tufa (a very porous rock), and here specimens of low-growing *Dianthus*, *Silene* and Saxifrages flourish. *Saxifraga longifolia* is a striking species which forms a fine rosette of silver leaves, up to 17cm across. It grows wild on limestone cliffs in the Pyrenees, and is especially common in the gorges north of Pamplona, growing on vertical limestone cliffs in company with the hardy gesneriad *Ramonda myconii* (this plant is also grown at Wisley – on the peat bank and rock walls). The rosette of *Saxifraga longifolia* grows for several years without flowering, and then exhausts itself with one magnificent pyramid of flowers, up to 50cm tall. It has to be reproduced from seed, but a hybrid, only slightly smaller, called 'Tumbling Waters' does produce offsets, and has persisted in cultivation since the 1920's. It is said to be a cross between *S.longifolia* and *S.callosa*.

At the southern entrance to the alpine area are two raised beds; the lower of these contains *Campanula*, *Erodium* and *Geranium* species and varieties, while the other houses daphnes, *Phlox*, *Dianthus*, dwarf hebes, and other interesting plants such as *Sorbus reducta*, *Aciphylla montana*, *Pulsatilla vernalis*, and *Euryops acraeus*. *Pulsatilla vernalis* is one of the most beautiful of alpine flowers, with its petals shining white inside, bluish and covered with rusty-brown hairs on the outside. It is tricky in cultivation, but succeeds well here, kept slightly moist in summer, and if possible, protected from rain in winter. In the Alps it usually seems to grow in gravel on moraines or in otherwise very well-drained places in poor soil: I have heard, however, that it can be magnificent when growing along the edges of mountain tracks in Norway, well-fertilised in spring with cow dung from the herds moving up to the alpine pastures.

Euryops acraeus grows wild on basalt cliffs in the high Drakensberg of Lesotho and Natal at an altitude of 2700 to 3300 m. It was originally misidentified as *Euryops evansiae*, but that is a distinct species, usually taller with larger leaves, smaller flowers, and narrower petals. About a hundred species of *Euryops* are known from southern Africa, but this is the hardiest, growing well outside in northeastern Scotland and surviving both frost and cold wind. It does, however, dislike heat and drought in summer. Unusually for a shrub, it can be propagated by both stem and root cuttings, and new plants may even appear where roots become exposed.

On each side of the site there is now a wide, sloping path, enabling visitors in wheelchairs and babies in pushchairs to visit the alpine area, something that was previously only possible after a long uphill push over grass.

The Rock Garden

The Rock Garden lies on a sloping site immediately to the north of the alpine area. Although there is plenty to see here throughout the year, it is probably at its most spectacular during April and May.

Messrs Pulham & Son, "Experts in Rock and Water Gardening", a well-known firm at the time, started work on this rock garden in January 1911, and many people will be amazed to learn that the entire construction was

A general view of the Rock Garden.

Water irises and Ragged Robin by the long ponds at the foot of the Rock garden.

completed by August of the same year! Further details of the building of it will be found on page 21. The stone originally used was Sussex sandstone from a quarry at West Hoathly; in the early 1960's, and again more recently, some reconstruction has been undertaken, using stone from the same quarry, and a scree area has been incorporated at the eastern end.

Two bold paths, traversing the rock garden at the highest and lowest levels, are linked by a series of small paths and rocky steps which meander upwards, allowing the visitor a close view of the small plants. A series of pools and waterfalls provide suitable conditions for moisture-loving plants, and the water eventually flows into the Long Ponds at the base of the Rock Garden and the Alpine Meadow.

Not surprisingly, the maintenance of the Rock Garden is a major task, and the permanent staff, augmented by students doing their practical work, are kept busy throughout the year – planting, hand-weeding, clearing out pools, and so on. In the past a number of well-known Wisley characters gave years of service. For example, Wynne Shepherd, (see opposite) worked solely on the rock garden for many years, weeding the beds, paths and rock crevices from one end to the other during the summer, and sowing seed in the winter. Ken Aslet, mentioned also on page 39, worked here, first as a foreman and later as superintendent, from 1949 to 1975. Ken, who is remembered with great affection by many of the RHS staff, would have been pleased to know that some of the materials used in the reconstruction of the alpine area (described below) were purchased with money donated to the fund set up in his memory. During his time at Wisley, Ken was responsible for the continued high standard of planting and the maintenance of the collections on the Rock Garden; he also instituted a number of changes and improvements. During the long hard winter of 1962, Ken and his team cleared a large area of *Rhododendron ponticum* that bordered the Wild Garden, removed vast quantities of infertile clay that had been dug from the ponds at the foot of the rock garden, and widened a drainage ditch that had been almost completely concealed by the Rhododendrons. They then converted the ditch and adjacent border into a bog and water garden, a feature that has now matured successfully.

In 1963, two new pools were added to the series of long ponds at the base of the rock garden, and over forty tons of new Sussex sandstone was used in the area above these two pools. By building up this new area, a large part of it became slightly south-facing, thus providing a much-needed sunny area in an otherwise north-facing site. Also at this time several new bridges were built over the stream using large flat slabs of stone, and these are still in place today. Prior to this, the stream was crossed only by stepping-stones. In Ken's own words:

"Some people have found the stepping-stones awkward to negotiate. All the original crossings of our stream were like this and it was very forcibly brought home to me one day that all was not well. I had gone down to collect some cuttings, and

A view of the Rock Garden, with Wynne Shepherd (see opposite) in the foreground.

Azaleas at the foot of the Rock garden.

turned round just in time to see an old lady tottering on a stepping-stone and to see her subside gently on her back in a shallow pool. I had to step into the water, lift her out and prop her up on a seat to drain off while we fished in the pool for her handbag and sent down to the office for first aid. We soon provided two alternative crossings by making bridges with very large slabs of stone.''

After Ken's retirement, his place as Superintendent was taken by John Warwick, himself now retired, and succeeded by Alan Robinson. Under these superintendents, and under the guidance of John Main, as Curator, reconstruction continued on a larger scale than before, with the result that a large area of the Rock Garden has only recently been replanted. A wide variety of alpines is to be seen, together with a number of dwarf trees including maples, conifers and one bonsai specimen – an ancient Japanese larch, which is well over 150 years old. Peat banks have been constructed at the western end of the rock garden and these provide a home for such plants as dwarf rhododendrons, hellebores, trilliums, Asiatic primulas, and *Nephrophyllidium crista-gallii*, a relative of bogbean, from Japan.

The bridge leading from the Rock Garden to the Wild Garden is draped with Wisteria floribunda f. macrobotrys, *a form with extra – long racemes of flowers.*

The Alpine Meadow

This adjoins the eastern end of the Rock Garden, and it is at its best during the spring. It is a grassy slope, with outcrops of rock (moved here in 1928) and a path meandering across it. During late March and early April there is a wonderful show of thousands of little hoop-petticoat daffodils, *Narcissus bulbocodium*. This very attractive daffodil is a native of southwest France, Spain, Portugal and North Africa, growing in a variety of habitats, but often in peaty moorland at high altitudes. It is therefore happy in fine turf which never dries out, and seeds itself freely here, as it does also at the Savill Garden, Windsor, where a paler yellow form is common.

Also naturalised in the meadow are dogs-tooth violets, *Erythronium dens-canis*, and the dainty *Crocus tommasinianus*, which has seeded itself so freely on the Rock Garden as to become almost a weed. *Narcissus*

The Alpine Meadow, with drifts of the little daffodil, Narcissus bulbocodium, *and an* Amelanchier.

Dogstooth violets, Erythronium dens-canis *and* Narcissus bulbocodium *in the Alpine Meadow.*

77

Primula *'Bonfire'*
makes a spectacular
display in the Wild
Garden in spring.

triandrus (a small species from Brittany, Spain and Portugal, which flowers from February to April) and blue wood anemones appear a little later. At the foot of the meadow is a bridge leading to the Wild Garden, and this is covered with the Japanese *Wisteria floribunda f. macrobotrys,* which looks marvellous in May when its long racemes of flowers hang down into the water.

The Wild Garden

The Wild Garden is the oldest part of the garden at Wisley; it was originally planted by Mr G.F. Wilson during the 1880's, and thus formed the nucleus of the garden when the Society took over the site in 1904. At that time, the area consisted of natural oak woodland, and here Wilson established lilies, *Cardiocrinum giganteum,* and many other interesting plants. For further details of the Wild Garden in Wilson's time see page 16.

Since that time, many changes have taken place, partly due to the growth (and latterly the downfall in the hurricane) of many of the trees and shrubs planted by Wilson, and partly due to the addition of many new species unknown to horticulture at that time. Recently, a considerable clearance has been made at the eastern end of this area, with the result that the visitor can catch a glimpse of Seven Acres (see below) through the trees in the Wild Garden. In the Wild Garden itself there are many interesting shrubs, amongst them the very beautiful *Magnolia sprengeri* var. *diva* (which received an Award of Merit in 1924) and *M.kobus*. The latter is a native of Japan, and although it does not flower freely when young, mature specimens are very floriferous; happily the tree in the Wild Garden is such a one! *M.sprengeri* var. *diva* is a natural variety, which was originally raised in 1900 from seeds sent back by the plant hunter. E.H. Wilson (not to be confused with G.F. Wilson!) from China. The flowers are a beautiful rosy pink on the outside, paler pink with darker lines on the inside, and are borne from March to April.

Other shrubs include *Corylopsis, Enkianthus, Pieris* and *Sciadopitys verticillata,* the umbrella pine. *Sciadopitys* was introduced to England in 1861, and it is interesting to note that a young plant was exhibited at the RHS on June 5, just a few days after its arrival from Japan.

A number of large old specimens of rhododendrons are to be found in the Wild Garden, amongst them the beautiful hybrid *Rh*. Sir Frederick Moore 'Coronation', named after a former Director of the Glasnevin Botanic Garden in Dublin; this flowers towards the end of April. *Rh.rex,* a species from Yunnan and Szechwan, was collected under the number 03800 by Joseph Rock, while *Rh.calophytum,* another species from Szechwan, was introduced by Wilson in 1904. A very large tree, this bears pale pink flowers in April, and two different forms have been given the Award of Merit and First Class Certificate respectively.

In early spring drifts of the little golden *Narcissus cyclamineus* (a native of Portugal and northwest Spain) cover large areas of the Wild Garden, and other small bulbous plants, such as snowdrops, anemones and *Erythronium americanum* and *E.revolutum* also thrive in the moist soil. As in Wilson's day, the blue poppy, *Meconopsis,* and many types of *Primula* do well, and hostas, hellebores and epimediums add to the variety in spring. The unusual yellow foxglove, *Digitalis lutea,* does well here, grown from seed collected by Christopher Brickell (Director General of the Society); it flowers in late spring, continuing until early summer.

Primula pulverulenta *in the Wild Garden.*

Euphorbia characias *subsp.* characias, *a spurge from the western Mediterranean, thrives in Bowles' Corner.*

Ferns are well represented in this area, liking the moist, shady conditions. They, and plants which associate well with them, are planted in a group with a path made of round sections of tree trunks winding through them, enabling visitors to see them closely.

As mentioned above, large numbers of Hostas and *Galanthus* are grown in this area, as they form part of the National Collections of these two genera, which are among several held at Wisley. The NCCPG (National Council for the Conservation of Plants and Gardens), an independent body whose headquarters are based in the building known as The Pines at Wisley, has set up a nationwide network of these reference collections, enabling professionals and amateurs alike to inspect, at one location, comprehensive collections of many of the popular plants and shrubs. Other collections held at Wisley include *Colchicum*, *Pulmonaria* and heathers. In some cases, this work is linked with that of the registration of plant names, and the work of the Registrar, Dr Alan Leslie, is discussed on page 61.

Two small areas of the garden are particularly worth a detour in spring – Bowles' Corner, and the peat beds on the north side of Weather Hill Cottage.

Bowles' Corner

This was created in 1958 in memory of E.A. Bowles (see also page 35), a great gardener and author of several books who gave invaluable help and advice, and years of service, to the Society. Bowles loved to grow 'curiosities' such

Right: *The epitome of an English spring– bluebells growing at the edge of Seven Acres.*

as the Corkscrew hazel *Corylus avellana* 'Contorta', which he described as *"the first crazy occupant (of my garden) and.. perhaps the maddest of all now"*, and this, along with a corkscrew willow and corkscrew hawthorn for company, were the first specimens to be planted there.

He also collected and raised a number of plants, many of which bear his name, and can be seen in Bowles' Corner. Examples include *Rheum palmatum* 'Bowles' Red', whose leaves are of a striking red colour when they first appear in the spring; *Vinca minor* 'Bowles' Variety', a low-growing periwinkle with bright blue flowers (collected near Grenoble); *Malus* 'Bowles' Hybrid', and Bowles's Golden Sedge, *Carex stricta* 'Aurea', a sedge which he collected in Wicken Fen in East Anglia. At the centre of this little garden is a glass case containing the small two-pronged fork which Bowles used so frequently to dig up treasures from his garden for his many friends; the fork, and a seat, were presented to the Society by Mrs Frances Perry on behalf of the Forty Hill Mutual Improvement Society, which Bowles had founded in 1910.

The Peat Beds

These, adjacent to Weather Hill Cottage, were constructed recently, and provide ideal conditions for primulas, dwarf rhododendrons, *Cyclamen, Gentiana sino-ornata* and the beautiful ice-blue *Primula bhutanica*.

From the Wild Garden one can follow the path into Seven Acres, via the Round Pond, or turn into the Walled Garden.

Seven Acres

The area lying between the Wild Garden, the River Wey, and the Restaurant is known as Seven Acres. It contains a small lake (originally a gravel pit), the heather garden, a wide variety of trees, shrubs and herbaceous plants, and a round pond which is a delight to children because of the large number of ducks and big carp which frequent it. On the banks of the Round Pond are established clumps of *Gunnera manicata*, a native of Brazil, whose enormous leaves start to unfurl in the spring. To avoid frost damage the large root crowns should be covered in the winter with bracken, straw, or its own old leaves. The royal fern, *Osmunda regalis*, is also well-established here; its elegant green leaves, tinted with a coppery hue, unroll in the spring and last through the summer until the autumn, when they become an attractive yellow and brown colour. Naturalised on the thick roots of the *Osmunda* is a most attractive colony of spring snowflake, *Leucojum vernum*. Near the pond, growing on the roots of an old *Acer rubrum*, is a spreading mat of *Lathraea clandestina*, a strange (some would say sinister!) parasite which bears bright purple flowers in early spring; it is a relative of the wild English toothwort.

The Heather Garden is described in the Autumn section of this book (see page 121), but there are some plants of interest here throughout the year; in spring, specimens to look out for include *Erica arborea, E.lusitanica*, and their hybrid *E.x veitchii*, and a tall, larger-flowered species from Spain called *E.australis*.

One of the most interesting features of the lake is the swamp cypress, *Taxodium distichum*, which stands on the little island close to the bank. On close inspection, it will be seen that the base of this tree is surrounded by curious woody 'knees'; it was once thought that the purpose of these protuberances was to supply trees growing in water with air, but it has recently been found that their removal makes no difference to the health of the tree – very disappointing! Quite apart from this remarkable feature, Taxodiums produce beautiful pale green feathery foliage in spring, are quite hardy, and can grow up to a hundred or more feet high – a beautiful tree, but strictly for the larger garden.

Elsewhere in Seven Acres are flowering cherries, crab apples, sweetly-scented lilacs and *Philadelphus*; all beautiful during the spring and early summer. Leaving aside the Pinetum and Howard's Field, which are described elsewhere, the best area to visit next is the Walled Garden, situated between the Wild Garden and the formal canal.

The Formal Garden

This area was designed by Lanning Roper in 1969, and is described on page 37. The enclosed garden to the west of the parallel yew hedges is at its best in summer, and is therefore treated on page 105. The area backing onto the open-sided pavilion (formerly the potting-shed) however, is usually very colourful in spring, being planted with a range of bedding plants and bulbs, such as tulips, wallflowers, pansies and forget-me-nots. From here, one has a good view over the canal to the southern face of the laboratory. This south-facing wall provides excellent shelter for many plants which are early-flowering, or of suspect hardiness. Of great beauty here in the spring are *Ceanothus papillosus*, and the very early-flowering China rose, 'Pompon de Paris' which grows through it. *Clematis montana*, and its deep pink form 'Tetrarose', grow on the corner of the Laboratory wall near the entrance. 'Tetrarose' is a robust, tetraploid variety with larger petals than the usual *C.montana*.

Spring bedding in the formal walled garden.

Summer

T O VISIT Wisley in the summer is to experience some of the finest aspects of English gardening. Some people have said that the garden is too impersonal and lacks the intimacy of a more diminutive private garden, but Wisley is composed of numerous smaller areas, and does not on the whole depend on long vistas or grand scenes for its effectiveness; furthermore, the model gardens (described on page 91) are intentionally built on a small scale. In contrast to the great botanic gardens, such as Kew and Edinburgh, plants at Wisley are grown not only for their botanical interest, but also for their ability to add colour (whether of flowers, foliage, bark or berries) and form to the garden. These plants are grown so that visitors can see them in a garden setting and learn how they could use the same plants in their own gardens.

Nearly all areas of the garden have something of interest to offer at this time of year, but the Summer Garden and the mixed borders leading up to Battleston Hill are at their finest; here can be seen an enormous range of herbaceous plants, mixed with annuals, biennials, bulbs and shrubs.

Roses, too, are at their best during late summer and autumn – at Wisley there are three major areas where they can be seen; along the western edge of, and in, the Summer Garden, in the Garden for New Rose Introductions, and in the main rose borders on Weather Hill. Roses are also trained on the walls of the Laboratory and the Formal Garden.

There is a great deal to see on the Portsmouth Field at this time of year; trials of ornamental plants are usually at their most spectacular, particularly the annuals and perennials, which should be at their peak. Vegetables can be seen also, both on the Portsmouth Field, and in the Model Vegetable Garden, and of course soft fruits, such as strawberries, should be in full production in the Model Fruit Garden.

A tranquil scene – waterlilies on the lake in Seven Acres.

The corner of the Laboratory, showing the sundial and rose 'Mermaid' on the wall.

Entrance and Main Terrace

To simplify matters as far as possible, we have described the various areas of the garden in more or less the same order in each of these seasonal sections – that is, as if the visitor were walking round in a roughly clockwise direction. Obviously, this will not suit everyone, so we draw the readers attention to the comprehensive index at the end of the book, which should enable him or her to find a reference to any part of the garden.

Passing through the main entrance, one sees, growing against the sunny, south-facing wall of the laboratory, the single deep yellow shrub rose 'Helen Knight', which was raised in 1966 from a seedling of *Rosa ecae* (a species from Afghanistan and Central Asia) growing on the wall of the Director's House at Wisley; Frank Knight, then Director, named it after his wife. 'Helen Knight' makes a bush up to three metres on a wall such as this, and the warmth of the wall provides the extra heat needed for it to flower freely.

On a sunny day, the visitor can check his watch against the sundial commemorating the first Superintendent of Wisley – S.T. Wright, the man responsible for moving the Society's plants from the earlier garden at Chiswick. Continuing up the short flight of steps, the main terrace is reached, and from here one can turn left into the Broadwalk, or carry straight on towards Weather Hill Cottage (private), before turning left into the summer garden.

Summer Garden

This garden, one of the more intimate areas at Wisley, has been planned to be at its peak in summer. It contains both old favourites, and new introductions. Some of these old garden flowers have recently regained their popularity, while some have never gone out of fashion. Among the reasons for the resurgence of such plants is their delicate beauty, allied to toughness of constitution – in contrast to some of the more coarse and colourful modern varieties, which may grow quickly, but frequently die equally quickly! Many of the older varieties have a strong scent, an attribute often lost in modern hybrids. Graham Stuart Thomas, formerly Gardens Advisor to the National Trust, has influenced the creation of this garden, and it has proved very successful and popular. He is the leading expert on old roses in England, and he generously gave stock plants of a number of them and of the rarer wild species to the Society; on the western side of this garden are a number of deliciously – scented roses, trained along post and wire fences. Among the specimens to be seen here are such elegant beauties as 'Amy Robsart', a *Rosa rubiginosa* hybrid raised by Lord Penzance in 1894. She bears small, single red flowers, with bright yellow stamens, in June; their scent is only faintly discernible. 'Lord Penzance' and 'Lady Penzance', appropriately enough, occupy adjacent positions, blooming companionably in July. Both hybrids of

R.rubiginosa, these were also raised by Lord Penzance in 1894; the single flowers of 'Lord Penzance' are a lovely apricot colour and are sweetlyscented while 'Lady Penzance' is slightly fragrant, with single pink flowers. It is interesting to note that the glands on the leaves of these Eglantine hybrids smell strongly of apples on a damp day, and it

Beds of Busy Lizzies and Helichrysum petiolatum *on the Main Terrace.*

The Summer Garden, with Lilium *'Enchantment', lavender and roses.*

is this, rather than the scent of the flowers, which is their special characteristic.

Alongside these roses are the sweetly-scented hybrid musks 'Felicia', with pale apricot double flowers; 'Penelope', with bright pinkish-orange buds followed by pale lemon – yellow flowers; 'Cornelia', which bears pale pink flowers in summer, and darker pink blooms in autumn; and 'Buff Beauty', with buff-coloured flowers which fade slightly in due course. All these are at their peak during high summer, although many of them have a second period of flowering throughout late summer and autumn. Within the garden itself are a number of symmetrically arranged beds, divided by grass paths, with an urn on a plinth providing a central focal point. This area has a very

The main rose borders, looking towards the Bowes Lyon Pavilion (see page 38).

"English" feel about it, with a tranquil atmosphere induced by the subtle harmonies of colour and scent. There are a number of shrub roses in the beds, providing an element of height, and some of these are really old varieties such as 'Conrad Ferdinand Meyer', a hybrid *rugosa* raised in 1899. It bears a large number of very fragrant, pale pink double blooms in early summer and again in September. 'Madame Pierre Oger', a Bourbon rose found in 1874 as a sport on 'La Reine Victoria', bears rounded, well-scented pale pink blooms with incurved petals from midsummer until autumn. Two more lovely old varieties deserve a mention here, 'Gloire des Mousseaux', a damask moss with sweetly-scented, double pale pink flowers produced in midsummer (occasionally it also produces a few extra blooms in the autumn), and 'Cécile Brunner', a miniature Hybrid Tea raised in 1881, which bears very pale pink, flowers in midsummer from tiny high bulbs.

Amongst the newer roses are 'Golden Wings', a hybrid of *R.pimpinellifolia* raised in 1956, with large, well-scented single yellow blooms produced almost continuously throughout the summer; and *Rosa moyesii* 'Geranium', which originated at Wisley as a seedling of *R.moyesii* in 1938. The commonest clone of *R.moyesii* in cultivation, 'Geranium' makes an open bush with rather stiff stems up to 2.5 metres high. The flowers are bright red and are succeeded by striking orange hips in September. There are many other plants of interest in this garden, not all of which can be mentioned here, but it is worth looking out for the collection of cultivars of *Phygelius*; many of the newer forms such as 'Moonraker' (a 'must' for James Bond fans!) and 'Cream Trumpet' are hybrids of *P.aequalis* and *P.capensis*, both species which grow by the edge of streams in the Drakensberg mountains of South Africa. Also from Africa are the daisy-like Osteospermums, which flower for months on end, beginning in midsummer, and continuing into autumn until the first hard frost. There are many hybrids, including the Wisley

Hybrids, 'Whirligig' and 'Cannington'; not surprisingly, considering their provenance, all these enjoy sun, as does the bush of the Spanish Broom, *Spartium junceum*, which produces its racemes of rich yellow, fragrant flowers from June to September. Other plants of interest include hardy fuchsias, aquilegias, kniphofias, irises, *Agapanthus*, potentillas and geraniums. In addition there are many good peonies, with a particularly fine specimen of *P.suffruticosa* 'Joseph Rock', thought to be close to the wild form of this species. The seeds were collected in the garden of a lamasery in northwest China by the great American plant collector, Joseph Rock in around 1932. In spite of its being so beautiful and sought-after, it is still very scarce in cultivation as it is so hard to propagate. To the south of this area is a collection of roses.

Garden of New Rose Introductions
This garden, first planted during 1973, contains groups of over two hundred different bush and climbing rose cultivars introduced during the last five years. The idea is to enable visitors to judge for themselves the performance of the newest roses; as the acid, sandy soil at Wisley is far from ideal for them, it means that one can see which roses perform well even in rather unfavourable conditions. Hybrid Teas (now known as large-flowered roses), floribundas (cluster roses), and climbing roses are all included, and each one is grown for five years after its introduction. New ground-cover roses, and a selection of David Austin's new English Roses are planted in special beds near the model vegetable garden.

If the cultivar is found to be particularly good, new stock is obtained at the end of the five – year period for planting in the main rose borders or elsewhere in the Garden; if it is not considered outstanding it is discarded to make way for another newly – introduced cultivar, thus ensuring that the collection is always up – to – date. A leaflet listing the new roses in this section and giving details of suppliers is available at the Information Centre. For many years,

until 1987, the rose collection was looked after by Sid Love, who will be known to many Wisley visitors and others, for his work as a flower arranging demonstrator.

Broadwalk
The Broadwalk leads south from the Main Terrace up towards Battleston Hill. On either side of the wide grass walk, edged with paving slabs, are two borders over a hundred and fifty metres long, and about seven metres wide. These two beds, known as the Mixed Borders, are backed by hornbeam hedges – one of the most satisfactory hedging plants (see also page 111). The Mixed Borders are so-called because of the mixture of plants which they contain: herbaceous perennials, shrubs (singly and in groups), ornamental grasses, and annuals.

Wisley's poor and very well-drained sandy soil requires heavy use of fertilisers and mulches; one which is often used on the roses and other areas of the garden where an acid soil is not needed, is mushroom compost, the manure which has been used to grow mushrooms, to which has been added much-needed chalk. Irrigation is often required in dry periods, and the gardens have permission to pump water out of the river Wey.

About every eight years or so, the entire collection of plants has to be removed and replanted, once the

The Broadwalk in summer – large clumps of herbaceous plants spill out over the paving, and in the background can be seen the tall grass, Arundo donax.

ground has been sterilised to kill weeds and bugs. This time-consuming operation has recently been carried out, so the borders should once again be spectacular, and more or less weed – free. Graham Stuart Thomas (already mentioned in connection with the Summer Garden) has drawn up new planting plans, with the emphasis more on herbaceous plants than before, and the first two phases, that is the end sections of the borders, have already been replanted (1989); the middle section of each bed will be planted up during 1990.

There is an enormous range of herbaceous plants to be seen here – peonies, irises, *Phlox*, *Kniphofia*, geraniums, lupins, daylilies, *Lychnis* and so on. There are one or two older specimens which have been retained from previous plantings, and notable amongst these is the very large clump (about three metres high) of *Paeonia lutea* var. *ludlowii* (A.M. 1954) which can be seen at the northern end of the borders. There are also two large clumps of dwarf pampas grass, *Cortaderia selloana* 'Pumila', four large stands of *Arundo donax*, looking rather like a slender form of maize, and two rather small (about three metres of a

possible thirty high at present!) clumps of the attractive hardy gum tree, *Eucalyptus gunnii*. These will probably be pollarded every other year so that they keep their attractive foliage.

Halfway up the Broadwalk, on the left-hand side, is a small semi-circular paved area, backed with high hornbeam hedges and containing a number of seats from which one has a good view over the Broadwalk and Colour Borders up towards the main rose walk and the Bowes Lyon Pavilion. In the centre of this area is a small specimen of the Maidenhair tree, *Ginkgo biloba*, which was presented to the Garden by a group of ex-Wisley students in 1983. The *Ginkgo* is a fascinating and rather beautiful tree, with very distinct leaves quite similar in shape to the maidenhair fern, *Adiantum* – hence its common name. It is the only living representative of a genus of very ancient trees and has survived almost unchanged since the carboniferous era, when much of the world was covered by swampy forests of giant ferns, cycads and horsetails. It is now unknown in the wild, but had survived in the gardens of Chinese temples before it was brought to Europe in around 1750. It is very hardy, long-

Clumps of Osteospermums, Artemisias, and Penstemons in the Broadwalk.

One of the model gardens – the Town Garden has been designed to cater for the needs of a young couple.

lived, and suffers from very few diseases and can eventually make a tree up to thirty metres high.

Looking at the names of plants in these borders, one is struck by just how many of the cultivars commemorate people, places, gardens and nurseries, some of them long dead and gone. In these borders alone one can see *Nepeta* 'Six Hills Giant' (nursery), *Potentilla* 'Abbotswood' (garden), *Artemisia* 'Powis Castle' (garden), *Kniphofia* 'Bees Sunset' (nursery), and *Sidalcea* 'Elsie Heugh' to mention but a few. To the southwest of the Broadwalk, lie the Model Gardens.

The Model Gardens

These have been laid out to illustrate the effects that can be achieved in a small space – roughly equivalent to the 'average' town or suburban garden of today – and they always seem to attract plenty of visitors, who are unable to resist making comments (both favourable and unfavourable!) on their design; presumably this is a good sign – many people obviously "identify" with them. Each plot is designed to appeal to a different group of gardeners, and each employs a range of buildings and paving materials that should be obtainable by the ordinary garden-owner.

We describe below the model gardens as they are at present (1989) – the Society is hoping to increase gradually the number of gardens to reflect presentday interests, and to widen the range of possible solutions to the problems of designing an interesting garden in such a small space. It is expected that these new gardens will be constructed on Weather Hill, near to the present site. The first three gardens described were sponsored by the Stanley Smith Horticultural Trust, a charity devoted to the improvement of horticulture.

The Town Garden was the first of these model gardens to be completed in 1976, and measures 22 by 7 metres –

large for Fulham, small for Clapham. It was laid out with the requirements of a young working couple in mind, and is specifically designed for all-year-round interest with easy maintenance. A hedge divides the garden, with a lawn on the house side, and a small greenhouse and patio with a table and chairs beyond.

The Family Garden (11 by 22 metres), is designed to accommodate sections for fruit and vegetables as well as a play area for the children and a colourful display of flowers. Efforts have been made to keep the basic fabric of the garden simple and reasonably economical, yet at the same time asthetically pleasing. Curving diagonal lines are employed in the path and borders to distract the eye from the rather severe, rectangular form of the plot. A clever idea is the small, shallow pool/sandpit which can be converted from one to the other according to the current state of the family's breeding programme. The flower and shrub beds that surround a small

The Enthusiasts Garden, showing the wide range of interesting and unusual plants that can be grown in a small space – in the background is the golden hop, Humulus lupulus *'Aureus'*

summer house and fruit cage at the end of the garden, contain many interesting plants which are easy to maintain and attract insects: butterflies visit the buddleias and the large pink sedums hum with bees, working frantically to gather some of the last nectar of summer. Every inch of space is used to good effect – climbers clothe the fence, and in the fruit area cordons and fan-trained trees are used to maximise the limited room.

Some idea of the enormous range of fruit that can be grown in a small space may be seen here; most of the apples are grafted onto 'dwarfing rootstocks' such as M26, which were raised at East Malling Research Station in Kent. (Further mention of this subject may be found on page 113 of the Autumn section). Against a larch-lap fence about five metres long and two metres high are trained no less than nine different cultivars, selected to produce fruit throughout the season. They range from 'Red George Cave', an early variety,

through 'Egremont Russet' (best eaten from October to December) to 'Sturmer Pippin', which can be stored until late spring. Adjacent to these apples are two vines, and the fruit cage contains a selection of gooseberries, redurrants and blackcurrants. On the opposite fence are trained cordon currants (white and red), gooseberries and pears, and there is also a fine fan-trained morello cherry.

Many of the vegetable cultivars have also been chosen for their compact habit – something which breeders have been working hard at for a number of years now, and there are plenty of useful ideas here.

The Enthusiasts Garden (15 by 23 metres) is, as the name implies, dedicated to the keen plantsman, and incorporates a number of microhabitats, enabling a wide range of interesting ornamental plants to be grown in a small space. Features include a small rock garden, peat beds, a drystone wall, pool, pergola, cold frame and greenhouse, with a raised bed running down the side of the plot to provide congenial conditions for those plants which appreciate a well-drained soil. Amongst the plants which thrive in the peat beds are *Dactylorhiza elata,* a large, handsome spotted marsh orchid from southwest Europe, various forms of *Rhodohypoxis*, *Arctostaphylos uva – ursi* (Bearberry), *Gaultheria procumbens,* and the dwarf rhododendrons *R. calostrotum* 'Gigha' and *R. campylogynum,* which has very aromatic leaves. On the fence near this area is the colourful deciduous climber, *Campsis radicans,* whose bright red and orange trumpet-shaped flowers are borne from August to September. Less well-known is its neighbour on the fence, *Alangium platanifolium,* a curious deciduous shrub from Japan and China, whose small white flowers are produced in June and July; an apt planting for this particular garden.

The Garden for Disabled People was planned in association with the Disabled Living Foundation, sponsored by Readers Digest, and constructed during 1977. It aims to show how gardens can be planned or adapted to suit the needs of those with a disability of some kind. Features such as raised beds, a small raised pool, a specially designed hexalight greenhouse, wide paths to allow for wheelchair access, and the use of ground-cover plants to avoid weeding, have all been incorporated, and it is hoped that the garden will encourage more disabled people to take up, or return to, gardening.

The Granada TV Garden

This was constructed, on the opposite side of the road to the gardens mentioned above, in 1984. It was designed specifically for use in a series of television programmes, entitled 'Gardeners Calendar' made by Granada TV, in conjunction with the RHS. In order that viewers would see the relevance of the programmes to their own gardens, it was essential that the majority of demonstrations should be filmed in a seemingly small garden, rather than in the main Garden itself. The site chosen is sloping, with a north-facing aspect, and measures about 15 by 8 metres overall.

David Mulford, Technical Assistant to the Curator at Wisley, was responsible for the construction of the garden and recalls, *"With each expert wanting maximum territory, some hard bargaining had to be entered into during which time boundaries vacillated with amazing elasticity. But always in the background was the need for an aesthetic entity."*

The Garden for Disabled People, which incorporates features such as raised beds and a raised pool.

The gazebo in the recently – created Scented Garden.

The Scented Garden

Unlike the other model gardens, in which the road is deemed to be the "house", it was necessary, for practical reasons, to treat the top of this site as the house, so some existing buildings which are offices for the garden staff were altered a little to lend credence to this idea.

The Scented Garden

This was only recently created, with donations from five countries in memory of Mrs Jean Cannon (1941 – 1986). It contains a range of plants with fragrant flowers or foliage, including roses, herbs, Viburnums and so on, set around a white gazebo which formed part of the Society's exhibit at Stoke Garden Festival in 1986. There are three small greenhouses within the garden, one of which contains a collection of Perpetual-Flowering Carnations, suitable for growing by amateurs; these are striking to look at, and have the most marvellous scent. As the name implies, they flower throughout the year, so a visit to this area is worthwhile at any time.

The Herb Garden

Whether or not this counts as a 'model garden' is rather a moot point, as one is unlikely to give over one's entire plot to herbs; nevertheless, many people will find it of interest, either as a design on which to base their own herb garden, albeit possibly on a smaller scale, or as a place in which many different kinds of herbs can be seen. Herbs have become increasingly popular in recent years, both for their culinary, cosmetic and medicinal uses, and also for their ornamental value. This herb garden was constructed during 1974/5, replacing the herb borders which had been next to the old Alpine House. It has generated a good deal of interest over the years, and aims to show a wide range of herbs, as well as traditional dye plants, which can be grown outside throughout the year. Half-hardy annual herbs such as Basil, *Ocimum basilicum*, are started indoors and planted out after all danger of frost is past. There is insufficient room here to go into details concerning all the species represented, but there is a Wisley Handbook, entitled *Culinary Herbs* which gives full descriptions and cultivation details for most of the herbs to be seen in the garden.

The Model Fruit Garden

This area contains a range of small model fruit gardens, a permanent wooden fruit cage, a strawberry plot, a number of demonstration plots, and areas for unusual fruits and experimental work. The model gardens are designed to show how the various methods of training fruit can be used to achieve high yields in a small space; most of the plants are grown on dwarfing rootstocks and in restricted forms such as cordons, fans or espaliers. Other considerations, such as spacing and choice of cultivars, are also taken into account, and for anyone planning a kitchen garden, this area is invaluable.

Of the model gardens, the smallest measures just 5 x 9 metres, of which 6 x 3.5 metres is given over to the cultivation of soft fruit. In this plot the east and west-facing fences are planted with cordon apples and pears, while the south-facing fence supports fan-trained peaches. Blackberries and the hybrid berries – Tummelberry and Tayberry, both raised at the Scottish Research Institute at Mylnefield on Tayside, are trained up a trellis archway, and raspberries, cordon gooseberries and red, white and black currants are grown in the centre of the plot.

In the next plot, measuring 9 x 9 metres, a wider range of bush, cane and tree fruits are grown, again showing the various methods of training, and here a board shows the average yields from each fruit – amazingly high in some cases, and certainly enough for the average family of four, although of course factors such as the age of the plants and the weather will account for some variation.

Another model garden is roughly the size of the average allotment, measuring 18 x 9 metres, and contains in addition to

The Herb Garden at Wisley contains a collection of culinary and medicinal herbs, and aromatic plants; in the foreground is variegated mint, Mentha rotundifolia 'Variegata'.

The Model Fruit Gardens contain many varieties of fruit trained in space-saving forms; these are pears, trained as cordons.

A view of the Model Vegetable garden.

the forms mentioned above a number of plum pyramids, a morello cherry and apples grown in "spindlebush" form.

In the demonstration plots unusual fruits such as blueberries, Chinese gooseberries (*Actinidia* species, also known as Kiwi fruit), and pot-grown apples are grown and evaluated; quite apart from their obvious advantages when grown in a small space, the latter look most ornamental.

Almost adjacent to the model fruit gardens is the Bowes Lyon pavilion (described on page 38), and from here one can look down the length of the main rose borders, towards the Broadwalk. These beds contain a massed display of Hybrid Tea and Floribunda roses, both new and old, making a magnificent sight in mid-late summer.

The Model Vegetable Garden

This is the preserve of one man, Colin Martin, who has worked in the garden since 1951, and whose family has a long association with Wisley; Colin was born in a cottage (since demolished) on Wisley Common, and in his spare time has built up a reputation as one of the most successful anglers on the nearby River Wey. It's his full time job to keep the vegetable garden in good order, and this he does admirably – it is always spick and span and full of the most mouth-watering produce. In addition to all the well-known varieties, numerous new cultivars of the common vegetables are grown, alongside less common delicacies such as Pumpkins, squashes and gourds, seakale, a range of Chinese greens, and different types of asparagus and artichokes. He experiments with cloches of varying designs, enabling visitors to see the amount of protection afforded by these, and is usually happy to give advice on the subject. Even for those people who are not particularly interested in vegetable growing, this garden is a delight to look at.

The 'Monocot' Borders

Sandwiched between the Model Vegetable Garden and the Alpine area, and backed by high yew hedges, are the 'Monocot' borders – so called because they contain a collection of monocotyledons (mainly the grass and lily families) and monocotyledon – like plants such as South American Eryngiums. South African plants in particular appreciate the relatively well-drained soil and sunny situation (quite a rare combination at Wisley) here, and the beds either side of the path are filled with species and forms of *Agapanthus*, *Kniphofia* (Red hot poker), yuccas, galtonias, phormiums, cardoons and other sun-lovers. The path slopes slightly towards the top of the rock garden and opens out at the end into a wider paved area from which one can look out over the Rock Garden and Wild Garden.

The Annual Beds

In summer it is worth returning from the model gardens to the service road via the Annual Beds, which are situated between the herb garden and the garden for the disabled. It is obviously impossible to describe the contents of these beds, since they change every year – the only permanent planting is several specimens of the weeping *Buddleia alternifolia*, a delicate small tree with cascades of pale mauve flowers and silver foliage.

Battleston Hill

By walking for a short distance in an easterly direction, one comes to the lower end of the central path on Battleston Hill, an area which was described on pages 66-70. Although Battleston Hill is particularly spectacular in spring, there are also several plants of interest here in the summer also. For example, there are a number of medium-sized bushes of hydrangeas, planted on either side of the main path, and most of these are in full flower from July until about September. Those represented here include *H.macrophylla* (also known as *H.hortensia*), a species from Japan and China, which has many small flowers borne in a flat or rounded inflorescence, and many of the garden forms and varieties derived from it. These can be roughly divided into two groups, the 'lacecaps', which are those varieties in which the flat inflorescence has a centre of the small fertile flowers surrounded by very showy ray-flowers, and the more common mop-headed type collectively called by gardeners (but not botanists!) 'hortensias'. A curious feature of these hydrangeas is that, with the exception of the white-flowered varieties, the colouring of the flowers is influenced by the acidity of the soil; on soils with a pH of less than 5.5 most cultivars are blue, whereas in areas with a pH of 7 or above they become pink. The soil on Battleston Hill is acid, with the result that most hydrangeas here are blue. Some of the varieties of lacecaps are very old – for example 'Veitchii', which was

A colourful display in the Annual beds on Weather Hill.

introduced in 1903 by the once-famous nursery of Messrs Veitch, and 'Mariesii', which was introduced from Japan by Charles Maries in 1879 and given the Award of Garden Merit by the RHS in 1938. Messrs Veitch, who sponsored many plant-collecting trips abroad during the latter half of the 19th century and the early years of this one had a hand in introducing another very fine shrub which can also be seen on Battleston Hill today- *Potentilla fruticosa* 'Purdomii' (also known as 'William Purdom'), one of the finest of the garden varieties of this species. Collected by William Purdom from Shensi in China in 1911 (on a visit sponsored by Veitch and the Arnold Arboretum in America) it makes a large, wide-spreading bush and bears canary-yellow flowers throughout the summer; it was awarded a First Class Certificate after trial at Wisley in 1966. Just over the brow of the hill, one sees the trials field.

The Portsmouth Field

Trials of plants have always constituted an important part of the Society's work – in 1818, when the Society's first little garden at Kensington was acquired, the Council announced that *"Experiments on the cultivation of particular Classes of Vegetables will (also) be carried on in the Garden under the direction of a Committee of Management"*. The first trials concentrated on fruit and vegetables, with dahlias and chrysanthemums being included at a later date. By 1860 the Superintendent of the Society's Garden at Chiswick was able to report to the Floral Committee that *"I have (also) sown upwards of three hundred kinds of annuals in pots, to be eventually planted out in the Experimental Flower Garden, for the purpose of having their merits tested by the Committee."*

Trials were (and still are) also carried out on less hardy plants, and in 1906, by which time the RHS had moved to Wisley, S.T. Wright was able to report that no fewer than 271 stocks of cannas, and 895 different cultivars of tulips, were being grown. Over the years since then, the Society has conducted trials on many thousands of ornamental plants and vegetables. The Portsmouth Field covers an area of 4¼ acres, and is a spectacular sight in summer; it was established as the site for all RHS trials (other than roses, rhododendrons, camellias and tender plants) in 1970. There are two groups of floral trials, known as 'Permanent' and 'Invited'. The permanent trials, as their name suggests, are continued from year to year; plants for inclusion in these trials are selected by one of the specialist committees, and are grown for comparison with a collection of standard cultivars maintained at Wisley. At present, permanent trials include border carnations, early-flowering chrysanthemums, delphiniums, dahlias, hemerocallis, irises, daffodils, pinks, and sweet peas. If, after a few years, plants are not recommended for an Award (see opposite) they are deleted from the trial, to be replaced by a newer variety.

The invited trials are those to which members of the Society, the horticultural trade and the public, are invited to send plants or seeds. These trials are usually of a relatively short duration, often testing annuals, and are frequently reviewed. Amongst the plants recently grown in invited trials are *Alyssum*, *Antirrhinum*, *Nicotiana*, petunias, and *Tagetes pumila*. Many annuals and biennials are grown, partly because the varieties available to the amateur are constantly changing, and the trials are

Trials in progress on the Portsmouth Field; here newly-planted chrysanthemums are irrigated.

one way of evaluating and demonstrating these. Stocks of many different kinds of vegetables are also grown in invited trials; in 1989 beet, cabbage, calabrese, marrow, parsnip, peas, potatoes and sweet corn were included. All trials are judged by appropriate specialist committees, whose members are acknowledged experts in their field, and who give their time and expertise to the Society free of charge. They normally inspect the trial several times during the flowering or fruiting season, and recommend awards, which are then confirmed by the Society's Council. Awards which can be given for this purpose are First Class Certificate, Award of Merit, Highly Commended, and Commended. These awards are well – known and regarded as significant by professional gardeners and nurserymen, and are a valuable guide to the amateur gardener too. Many well-known gardening books and nursery catalogues (for example,

Hillier's Manual), when referring to a shrub or plant, will include the abbreviated form (i.e. F.C.C. etc.) of any RHS award that the plant has received. This is often followed by the date of the award, although this is not usually of any particular significance, but is of historical interest. These awards may have been given after a trial at Wisley or may have been awarded to the species or cultivar on the strength of a plant exhibited to the relevant committee at a London Show; where the letter 'T' appears after an award it donates "after trial at Wisley" (e.g. *Potentilla fruticosa* 'William Purdom' FCCT 1966). Again, the idea is to provide guidance for the Society's members, and other visitors to the Garden; reports of all trials are published annually in *Proceedings of the Royal Horticultural Society*.

The Jubilee Arboretum

This newish feature lies to the south-west and west of the Portsmouth Field,

A trial of delphiniums – note the wide range of colours available.

and is approached through a gap in the shelter belt of large trees that protects this end of the trials area. Thirty-two acres of undulating land, previously let for farming, was taken into the Garden in 1978 to commemorate the Silver Jubilee of the reign of Her Majesty Queen Elizabeth II. The Arboretum was officially opened by Her Majesty and HRH Prince Philip, who planted the first two trees, a pair of fastigiate purple beeches, *Fagus sylvatica* 'Dawyck Purple', either side of the entrance. An avenue of limes leads from the entrance to an English oak, planted in memory of Bert Pùllinger, a large and friendly man who worked at Wisley for more than fifty-two years, latterly mainly as the driver of the RHS lorry used for transporting plants to and from shows. Over four hundred trees have already been planted, and the work is by no means finished; planting an arboretum is a long-term venture. This area is totally exposed to the south-westerly winds, with the result that many of the young trees have not become established as soon as was expected; in an effort to speed up the growth of the specimen trees some fast-growing trees and shrubs have recently been planted to form shelter belts along the boundaries, and at intervals throughout the area. When complete, the arboretum will curve right round the south and west boundaries of the garden, as far as the end of the path at the foot of the rock garden, creating an attractive and interesting walk around the perimeter. The Arboretum is intended to be both of educational and aesthetic value; three main planting themes have been used – a series of seasonal walks, with trees grouped according to the season in which they are at their peak; clumps of trees selected for particular characteristics such as attractive and unusual bark, fastigiate or weeping growth, and so on; the third type of planting involves collections of all the species and cultivars of small genera. Most of the trees here are deciduous, as evergreens are well-represented in the Pinetum and elsewhere, although there is a small group of hollies at the far end of the east-facing field. A collection of fastigiate forms of various species can be seen at the bottom of the field to the left of the main entrance – amongst them *Quercus robur* 'Fastigiata', an upright form of the common oak, two maples (*Acer platanoides* 'Columnare' and *A.saccharinum* 'Pyramidale') and a particularly upright form of *Ginkgo biloba* (see also page 90). Above the Arboretum along the crest of the hill, is the Fruit Collection, which is described in the 'Autumn' section of this book (page 111); there is at present no access to this from the Arboretum. Assuming that the visitor has walked the whole way round the Arboretum, he or she will find himself arriving (much fitter!) at the bottom of the Rock Garden. The Rock Garden was fully described in the previous section (see pages 73-76) and there is of course much to be seen here during the summer months.

To the north is the Wild Garden, described on pages 78-82, which is pleasantly cool and shady on a hot day. Particularly attractive here during early summer are the Kalmias, hardy evergreen shrubs with beautiful bowl-shaped, usually pink, flowers. One, *Kalmia latifolia* forma *myrtifolia* is particularly striking here – it is a neat shape, with, as the name suggests, small leaves like those of a myrtle, and strangely contorted branches; its flowers are slightly smaller than those of the normal form, and it has been found that this dwarfism is controlled by a single recessive gene. Other dwarf cultivars have been raised in the U.S.A. with names such as 'Elf', pale pink, and 'Minuet' with red-banded flowers. There are now many other colour forms available in North America (its native country) with flowers of varying shades and unusual markings.

Seven Acres

This, the largest area of lawn and open space at Wisley, is situated on the northern side of the Wild Garden.

Here can be seen the Heather Garden (which will shortly be moved to a new site in Howards Field, see pages 121-122), the lake and the Round Pond.

On the side of the Round Pond nearest to the restaurant is a bed with a large collection of daylilies, *Hemerocallis*, both species and hybrids, interplanted with asters. Daylilies (popularly known as such because individual blooms last just one day but are succeeded daily by others) deserve a special mention because they are one of the comparitively few herbaceous plants which not only do not require frequent division and replanting, but positively thrive and increase in size if left to their own devices; add to this the fact that many of them have extremely attractive flowers and one can see why they are so popular. Many of the newer cultivars originated in the United States, and there are now such a huge number available that the RHS has in recent years held trials of them at Wisley in order to assess their merits. Daylilies are not fussy – they will grow equally happily beside water or in the herbaceous border – and last well when cut for flower arranging. There is insufficient room here to describe more than a few good ones which can be seen in this bed; 'Lemon Bells' (FCCT 1981), with yellow petals, brown on the reverse; 'Burning Daylight' (FCCT 1963), rich orange; 'Golden Chimes' (FCCT 1963), small golden-yellow flowers freely produced on a neat little plant. For those who wish to pursue the matter further, there is a British Hemerocallis and Hosta Society (President, C.D. Brickell, Director

The Round Pond, framed here by a fine plant of Gunnera manicata.

Scarlet daylilies, pink phlox, purple lythrums and red polygonums in Seven Acres.

General of the RHS) which can be contacted through the RHS office, and publishes a yearly bulletin.

Seven Acres is a much-visited area of the garden, probably due, at least in part, to its proximity to the restaurant; the heathers, together with many of the other shrubs in this area are in the process of being propagated in preparation for gradual replacement or relocation. A small path, alongside the River Wey, leads from Seven Acres to Howards Field, an area which lies between the pinetum and the Director's House (private); this part of the garden suffered serious damage in the hurricane of October 1987 and is being redesigned and replanted. The pinetum is fully described in the Winter section of this book (page 57), although it is of course equally interesting during the summer months.

Returning from the Pinetum, past the restaurant (which has recently been considerably enlarged, and serves – the authors can testify – excellent food and drink), one passes Aberconway House, the student hostel, which was officially opened in 1954 by the Queen Mother. The rather drab brick walls of this building have been much improved by the addition of a number of climbing plants, which thrive in this west-facing situation. Notable here are the repeat-flowering climbing floribunda rose 'Pink Perpetue', and *Ceanothus sorediatus,* a white-flowered deciduous shrub from western North America. By

Robinia hispida grows happily on the outer wall of the Walled Garden.

103

Actinidia chinensis *enjoys the sunny position on the west-facing wall of the Laboratory.*

passing the bed of ornamental grasses (described on page 123), and continuing in a westerly direction back towards the Wild Garden, one can enter the Walled Garden, via a pair of wrought-iron gates, erected in memory of Frank Knight, Director of Wisley from 1956-1969 (see also pages 34 & 37).

The Walled Garden

This garden, designed by Lanning Roper (see page 37) is at its best in summer, containing as it does herbaceous plants such as geraniums, phlox and erysimums, irises, old shrub roses and silver and grey-foliaged plants. There is a small central pool with a fountain, and around this are arranged beds surrounded by paved paths. On the walls are some very striking large ivies, notably *Hedera canariensis* 'Variegata' (also known as 'Gloire de Marengo'), which has cream-margined leaves with a central grey-green blotch, and *H. colchica* 'Sulphur Heart', whose leaves have bright central splashes of gold. On the south-facing wall is *Holboellia latifolia*, an evergreen climber from the Himalayan region, which produces its sweetly-scented flowers (male white, female purplish) during late spring and early summer; unfortunately it is not reliably hardy in the colder parts of Britain. Nearby is a small specimen of another Himalayan – *Piptanthus laburnifolius*, whose pea-shaped bright yellow flowers are also borne in early summer; again it is of doubtful hardiness, and often dies in very cold winters. A little later in the season two near neighbours, also on this south-facing wall, come into their own – the climbing rose 'Coral Dawn', whose large flowers blend well with those of *Clematis* 'Perle d'Azur'.

The Walled Garden is separated from the Formal Garden by a pair of high clipped yew hedges, at one end of which is another wrought-iron gate, this time commemorating W.D. Cartwright, a member of the Wisley staff for forty-four years. At the other end is a small gazebo, over which are trained the well-known *Rosa filipes* 'Kiftsgate', the climbing tea rose 'Lady Hillingdon', whose richly-scented, apricot-coloured flowers continue from midsummer into winter, and the cream-coloured hybrid musk 'Felicité et Perpetue'.

The Formal Garden

The Formal Garden gets its name from the formal beds which are filled with bedding plants; there is usually a very colourful display in this area, with winter and spring bedding schemes of wallflowers, pansies or forget-me-nots, underplanted with tulips, followed in summer by more tropical annuals and foliage plants. A mass of pale-pink *Cleome* was very beautiful here. The walls house more roses and other interesting climbing plants, such as *Schisandra glaucescens*, which bears orange-red flowers during May and June, and the hardy yellow-flowered perennial gourd, *Thladiantha dubia*. Leaving this area via the old potting shed, one can look out over the Formal Canal. A path passes along the north side of the water, with a mixed border alongside planted with fuchsias, roses, peonies, irises, buddleias and so on. On reaching the laboratory it is worth having a look at the plants growing on, and in the shelter of, the walls – these include *Azara serrata*, *Actinidia kolomikta*, *Ceanothus* 'Puget Blue', *Diascia vigilis*, and a fine specimen of *Fremontodendron* 'California Glory' growing next to rose 'Mermaid'. Also of interest are *Ceanothus* 'Trewithen Blue', *Carpenteria californica* and *Solanum crispum* 'Glasnevin'.

The Formal Canal, seen from the Laboratory.

Autumn

THE AUTUMN colours of native trees in England do not compare with those of North America, Japan, or even Scotland, either for splendour or sheer quantity. The cool summers and rich soils of most areas do not favour the production of bright reds and yellows; wild cherries and field maples which do often colour orange or red are relatively rare, and most native trees die off in shades of rich brown.

Wisley, in contrast, is a fine sight in autumn with many exotic trees and shrubs turning a fine colour before losing their leaves. The poor soils and generally warm summers of this part of Surrey are good for autumn tints, and in addition there are many fine specimens of trees notable for their good colouring. By the lake in Seven Acres is a particularly shapely young tree of *Nyssa sylvatica*, its lowest branches sweeping the ground; it never fails to turn brilliant red and orange. Nearby is a fine *Liquidambar*, with maple-like leaves turning purple and finally rich red.

The Wild Garden contains many well-coloured shrubs. The Highbush blueberries, *Vaccinium corymbosum*, provide delicious fruit, as well as good red and yellow foliage in autumn, and a large specimen of the Japanese maple 'Senkaki' turns brilliant yellow in October, remaining spectacular in winter with its crimson twigs. There is also a planting of Japanese maples, including *Acer japonicum* and *A. palmatum*, along the top of the Alpine Meadow; these are among the most beautiful trees for acid soils.

One of the special features of Wisley is the bulbs and other flowers naturalised in the Alpine Meadow. Particularly spectacular here in autumn are the crocuses and colchicums, and these are described on page 116.

Another spectacular feature in autumn is the Heather Garden, where hundreds of different species and cultivars of heaths and heathers are planted in drifts. This is described on page 121.

Cotinus coggygria, the Venetian sumach, makes a fine sight in autumn; here it is seen in Seven Acres.

The first striking plant that the visitor sees, on arrival at the main entrance of the garden, is a fine specimen of *Colquhounia coccinea,* an unusual sage-like shrub from the Himalayan region. This upright but rather leggy bush produces beautiful orange-red, funnel-shaped flowers from late summer into autumn, and thrives here on the sunny, south-facing wall of the Laboratory.

From here one walks along the main terrace and up into the Broadwalk, or into the Summer Garden, which, in spite of its name, also contains much of interest in the autumn; for example, many roses are still flowering vigorously, and in a favourable year, may continue to do so until Christmas. Those which are trained on the post and wire fence on the western side of this area are always good in autumn; 'Felicia', a beautiful apricot-coloured hybrid musk, is particularly floriferous, and 'Buff Beauty', 'Cornelia', and 'Penelope' are also well worth seeing. By September some of the earlier flowering

Hips of Rosa moyesii *'Geranium', a clone which originated at Wisley in 1938.*

roses have started to produce hips, which can be extremely decorative. One particularly attractive form is *R.multiflora* 'Placet', which has small leaves and tiny orange hips – both leaves and hips stay on for much of the winter.

Other good plants in the summer garden are the South African daisies, such as *Osteospermum* 'Whirligig', 'Cannington', and 'Killerton Park', *Argyranthemum frutescens* 'Jamaica Primrose' and 'Ochroleuca', and *Gazania uniflora* and 'Michael', which are at their best after a warm sunny season. Another South African, *Dierama pulcherrimum,* displays its graceful bell-like flowers from summer into the beginning of autumn; 'Blackbird', one of the many forms raised by the Slieve Donard Nursery in Northern Ireland, grows happily here, its violet-mauve blooms swaying gently in the breeze. Also from South Africa is *Anisodontea capensis,* an unusual small-leaved shrub, with magenta flowers, while from Mexico comes the beautiful *Salvia*

fulgens, a sun-loving species; the large, bright red flowers are produced in summer, and some linger on until September.

The Colour Borders

The contents of these borders vary from time to time, but at the moment they are planted with Michaelmas Daisies and other autumn-flowering herbaceous plants, mostly having flowers of mauve or purple colouring. Amongst the asters are *A.ericoides* and its cultivars 'Silver Spray' and 'White Heather'; *Aster laterifolius,* and a large specimen of *A. laterifolius* 'Horizontalis'. Also to be seen here is *A.simplex* var. *ramosissimus,* in which the individual flowers are tiny, but produced in such numbers that they give a fine misty effect. Other pink or purple plants include the well-known *Sedum* 'Autumn Joy ('Herbstfreude'), *Penstemon* 'Garnet', and *Liriope muscari. Colchicum speciosum* var. *album,* is, as the name implies, a white form of the *Colchicum* which is found in the Black Sea region. There are incidentally, many other specimens of these beautiful bulbs to be seen around the garden, particularly in the area between the walled garden and Weather Hill Cottage where a collection of different species and cultivars, including *C.atropurpureum* and *C.tenorii* and *C.intermedia* 'E.A.Bowles' has been planted.

The Broadwalk

Many of the plants in the herbaceous borders either side of the path will still be worth seeing during the early autumn, but there is no doubt that, on the whole, herbaceous borders begin to look a little sad after about the beginning of October. Naturally, the weather has a good deal to do with the way in which plants keep flowering late in the season, and if there has been a warm sunny summer this will help to encourage flowering to continue. Although the Broadwalk has recently been completely replanted there should still be plenty of colour to see in the latter part of the autumn, both from late-flowering perennials and from annuals and half-hardy bedding plants which are put in, to fill any gaps that may appear in the summer.

Battleston Hill

The majority of plants on Battleston Hill are spring-flowering, but, as mentioned previously (page 97), there are a number of good hydrangeas in this area, some of which will still be flowering in September and October. One such, 'Burgundy Lace', is a particularly attractive form of *Hydrangea paniculata,* a tall-growing species from Japan, Sakhalin and China. Another late-flowering cultivar is the aptly-named 'Tardiva', whose qualities can be judged by the fact that it has received both the Award of Merit and the First Class Certificate. Another eye-catching plant in September and October is *Cimicifuga simplex* 'Elstead, which makes a large clump by the side of the main path on Battleston Hill. This hardy herbaceous plant grows to about four feet high, has purple leaves and buds and produces feathery racemes of white flowers; other members of the family are similar, but usually flower a little earlier. A peculiarity of 'Elstead' is that, to my mind, it smells of coffee, although as an addict that may be just wishful thinking! Late- flowering hostas include 'Royal Standard', a hybrid of the scented *H.plantaginea.* There are a few small Japanese maples in this area, whose colour is always a delight in autumn, and one to note particularly is *Acer palmatum* 'Senkaki', which has lovely orange-red bark and bright yellow foliage.

The Portsmouth Field

During the autumn there is still much to see on the trials field, and it might surprise readers to learn that seed-sowing may occasionally still be seen in November! The most recent example of this unseasonal activity occurred when broad beans were sown on November 11, 1985; by choosing a warm, well-drained, sheltered site it is possible to plant beans that will withstand the winter weather in the south and produce a crop in June. Depending on the year's trials programme vegetables such as broccoli, cabbage, celery, carrots, Florence fennel, and sweet corn should still be in full production. Invitations for next years trials are posted annually in *The Garden*, usually in October and November, and detailed reports of all trials are published annually in *Extracts from Proceedings*. These reports are invaluable to amateur gardeners as they show not only which cultivars performed well under trial, but also give exact dates for sowing, transplanting, first flowering, etc. and even the compost mix used. Bertie Doe, supervisor of the vegetable trials department for thirty-three years prior to his retirement in October 1987, has been succeeded by Mr Reg Perryman (see below). Mr Doe, a charming and knowledgeable man, and an Associate of Honour of the Society, became well-known to television viewers of the 'Gardener's Calendar' series, and was a link with the 'old school' of gardeners who learned their craft on the job. He spent all of his working life in Surrey, first as a garden boy at Pyrford Court, and later as a head gardener near Godalming, before joining the staff at Wisley.

On the ornamental side, there should still be plenty to see during September; in 1986, for instance, there were trials of tobacco plants (*Nicotiana*) and snapdragons (*Antirrhinums*), and in both groups there were many cultivars which were still flowering at the time of the committee's final inspection in mid-September.

Chrysanthemums and dahlias, which are permanent trials at Wisley, usually form the main display on the Portsmouth field at this time of year. The first hard frost blackens the dahlias, but the chrysanthemums are hardier. In both these groups the roots are brought under cover for the winter; the dahlia tubers are usually replanted in spring, while the chrysanthemums are repropagated each year from cuttings produced from the roots in spring. The RHS has, almost since its inception, taken an interest in dahlias and chrysanthemums; by 1824, the Society was growing twenty-seven different kinds of the latter introduced from China, and when, in 1843 Robert Fortune was commissioned by the Society to travel to China in search of rare plants, he brought back many more types. The first Chrysanthemum Society was formed in 1846, and this eventually became the National Chrysanthemum Society, jointly with whom the RHS committee judges the trials of these plants at Wisley. One of the reasons for the popularity of the chrysanthemum is that it can be grown both indoors and out by the amateur with relative ease – by a judicious selection of cultivars flowers can be had from mid-summer until Christmas. It is probably at its most valuable during the autumn, when most other flowering plants are past their best; this is true not only in the garden, but also for decoration in the house, where they last exceptionally well as cut flowers. There are many different types of chrysanthemum available nowadays, and we do not have room to list them all here; instead we would recommend the Wisley Handbook *Chrysanthemums and Dahlias* which makes an ideal introduction to these plants.

In overall charge of the Trials programme is Mrs Sheila Ecklin, the Trials Recorder, who, with an office staff of three, is responsible for organising entries for trials and, in consultation with Mr Perryman, for arranging the dates on which the committees will first meet to inspect the plants; this in itself is no mean feat, bearing in mind the vagaries of the English weather. Mr Perryman, Trials Superintendent, oversees the cultivation of all ornamental and vegetable trials on the Portsmouth Field, and he and Mrs Ecklin both attend all committee meetings.

Wisley staff occasionally give demonstrations of various skills, and one that is popular in autumn is that covering digging, manuring and composting; this is normally given by Reg Perryman. Demonstrations are for the benefit of members of the Society, and their friends, and a limited number of tickets (for which no charge is made) are

The Hedge and Ground Cover Demonstration Area; in the foreground on the left is Cedrus atlantica *f.*glauca.

available in advance from the office at Wisley. Other subjects often covered include propagation, pruning, pests, diseases and disorders of fruit, vegetables and ornamental plants, glasshouse equipment, growing grapes, construction and planting of sinks and troughs.

In addition to the demonstrations listed above, Garden Walks are arranged for members, each of whom may bring one friend (with the exception of Sundays); there are usually one or two such walks a month, and different themes are followed, according to the season. For example, in September the fruit department is of special interest, in October particular attention is paid to autumn colour, and in November chrysanthemums and other plants in the glasshouses are inspected. Attendance at these walks is by ticket only, and the dates are published in advance in *The Garden.*

Hedge and Ground-Cover Garden

This area, situated to the west of the main glasshouse range, is of consider-able interest to anyone who is about to plant a new hedge in their own garden. A whole range of shrubs and trees, and other plants, some well-known as hedging material, and some not, can be seen here. The area has been developed since 1980, so the amount of growth since that time gives a good idea of the results that can be expected over a few years. Some of the more unusual choices are extremely successful, such as the Atlas Cedar, *Cedrus atlantica f. glauca,* which also has the benefit of being able to tolerate a high level of pollution, such as one might have to contend with in a city garden; it should, however, be borne in mind that, in due course this will make a very high hedge indeed! Ground-cover plants are established between the various hedges, and, again, these are useful for ideas; one cannot really describe this part of the garden as beautiful, since it is not "designed" – it is purely educational, and fulfils that function very well.

The Fruit Collection

Since its formation, the Society has always taken a considerable interest in the cultivation of fruits of all types; according to the *Catalogue of Fruits cultivated in the Garden of the Horticultural Society of London at Chiswick,* published in 1826, over 3,825 kinds of fruit (as well as "1,000 more, of less certain authority") were grown at one time. Depending on the Society's finances, larger or smaller collections of fruit have been grown, and experimental work carried out; for many years the National Fruit Trials were based at Wisley.

The present fruit collection is housed on a sixteen-acre site between the model fruit gardens and the Jubilee Arboretum. It includes ten acres of apples, many of which were planted during the late 1940's, and are divided into dessert and culinary types. Within this division they are further divided into groups, according to their season of ripening. Over 650 different apple cultivars are represented here, including a number of virus-free types grown on a rootstock known as 'Malling 26' (a method of controlling the size of the tree). All the 'old favourites' and many of the newer cultivars can be seen here, and although the official fruit trials, which were sited at Wisley until 1960 (see page 25 for further details) are now no longer carried out here, new varieties are frequently added to bring the collection up to date. In addition to apples, pears (ninety cultivars), plums and gages (ninety cultivars), currants, and other soft fruits are grown. In the autumn, when the fruit is harvested, a certain amount is sold to visitors at the entrance to the garden.

Harvesting apples in the Fruit Field.

One area of the fruit collection, the small vineyard, has attracted particular attention in recent years. With a growing number of commercial vineyards in Britain, and an increase in wine drinking in the population as a whole, more and more people are interested in trying to grow grapes, both for wine-making and dessert. Here at Wisley, a wide range of types of vine can be seen, and the fruits inspected, and a Wisley Handbook, *Grapes Indoors and Out*, describes the methods used to produce fruit both outside and under glass.

Fruit identification

Harry Baker, a fount of knowledge and the Society's Fruit Officer since 1969, is in charge not only of the fruit collection described above, but also of the model fruit gardens, demonstrations, and the business of fruit identifications – one of the Society's most popular services. Private gardeners are able, on payment of a small charge, to send in specimens of any fruit, together with a sample of shoot and foliage, and, all being well, obtain an identification – in a good season about 2,500 varieties may be sent or brought during the space of 20 weeks or so, and they can be seen lining the corridor waiting for attention: for more details of this service, write to The Director (Fruit Naming), RHS Garden, Wisley. Harry Baker keeps a reference set of apples from the Fruit Collection for comparison of the less common varieties. Most submitted are well known, but occasionally rare fruits from the dim distant past are sent in, for example the Costard, known in the 13th century, from which the name Costermonger was derived.

Meteorological station

Since 1826, when it was first considered desirable to observe the weather at its garden at Chiswick, the Society has kept daily meteorological records. The weather station was for some time situated at the top of Weather Hill (hence the name), but is now situated to the left of the main walk through the fruit collection, and is equipped with a barometer, sunshine recorder, rain gauge, thermograph, soil and air

A fallen giant: this Chamaecyparis, *growing on "the Graveyard" was one of the many trees that fell victim to the great storm in October 1987.*

thermometers and a Stevenson screen. Readings of these instruments are taken daily, and monthly reports are sent to the Meteorological Office at Bracknell, where they are used as part of the agricultural meteorological scheme. A synopsis of the year's weather at Wisley is sometimes published in *The Garden*, and students and research workers may consult the records, after making an appointment. Wisley, being low land within the valley of the River Wey, can sometimes suffer from very sharp frosts – the chief reason for moving the National Fruit Trials from the Garden to Brogdale – and over the years a few incidences of freak weather conditions, including a tornado and severe flooding, have also been recorded. These pale into insignificance, however, when compared to the storm of 16th October 1987, which wreaked appalling damage on the garden. The winds on that day gusted to nin miles per hour and more (the maximum could not be measured by the weather station) and the results of the impact on the garden can still be clearly seen. (See also pages 42 – 43).

The Model Fruit gardens

These were described on pages 95 – 96, and they are of especial interest in the autumn. Apples and pears should be in full bearing now, and it is amazing to see how many fruits a small spindlebush can support! In fact, it is worth mentioning here that the spindlebush is admirably suited to the cultivation of fruit trees in a limited space; the system involves a minimum of pruning and maximum early cropping, which helps to control the shape and vigour of the tree. Spindlebush training is not a new idea – the *Fruit Year Book* published by the RHS in 1950 included a paper, translated from the German, which described the spindlebush as an ideal form of tree for amateurs and commercial growers. For those who wish to learn more, detailed notes on the training of spindlebushes, as well as all other hardy fruits, can be found in *The Fruit Garden Displayed*, published by the Society.

The pot-grown apples are particularly elegant at this time of year – notably 'Spartan', whose fruits are a beautiful dark red, and 'Gala', which is orange. In this area too, can be seen a number of autumn-fruiting raspberries; these have attracted a good deal of attention with the introduction of new varieties in recent years, as, by fruiting from about the end of August until the first frosts in November or so, they extend

Columnar apples, growing in one of the model fruit gardens.

Above right: *Fruit trees in pots, seen here in one of the model fruit gardens.*

considerably the season during which raspberries can be harvested from the garden.

The Model Vegetable Garden

The model vegetable garden (as described earlier on page 96) is a cheering sight throughout the year – it doesn't look 'end-of-seasonish' (as our garden does in the autumn), but well-kept, and full of promising new delicacies to see the household through the winter. Amongst those of particular interest are the rarer root crops such as Chinese artichokes; unlike other artichokes which are of the daisy family, this is related to Deadnettle, being a species of Woundwort (*Stachys*). Other striking vegetables which are usually grown are purple Brussel Sprouts and a range of unusual varieties of endive.

Other model gardens

It is worth looking briefly at the model gardens at this time of year, partly because there are some late – flowering and foliage plants which are attractive, and partly because the 'bones' of the

gardens show up well when the eye is undistracted by a great display of colour. The fruit area in the 'family' garden (see page 92) is in full bearing now, so this is a good time to see just how much can be obtained from well-trained bushes.

The Glasshouses

These are fully described in the first section of this book (pages 47-50), but we shall mention them briefly here, as there is so much to be seen during the autumn. One of the most popular displays at this time of year is that of chrysanthemums, which are at their peak under glass during November. Various types, including cascade, charm and spray varieties, are to be seen in the cool section of the main glasshouse; the charms and cascades are grown out of doors until late September, when they are brought indoors, while the sprays are either treated in the same way, or grown entirely under glass. Whichever way is chosen, a remarkable display results, with an enormous number of blooms per plant. In the autumn of 1988, for example, there was a wonderful collection of the variety 'Blanche Poitevine', a very old dwarf, bushy cultivar, in the entrance porch of the greenhouse complex – these plants had an average of forty to fifty blooms per pot – now there's a houseplant worth having! Another interesting display during that autumn was a group of carnivorous plants; these were situated in the corridor leading off from the temperate section of the large glass-house, but can normally be seen in a small greenhouse just nearby. This display brought them to the visitors attention, and showed just how weird and wonderful they are.

An unusual plant which inhabits the same corridor, but is a climber, is the snail flower, *Phaseolus caracalla*, so called because of the snail-like shape of its coiled flowers. These are borne in the autumn, on pendulous racemes and are sweetly-scented and creamy white (ageing to pale orange) shaded with purple. This strange plant is believed to be one of the earliest exotics introduced into Britain, having apparently been grown in Hampton Court as early as 1690.

Other exotic plants which are worth seeing in early autumn include *Thunbergia grandiflora*, a vigorous evergreen climber with beautiful pale blue flowers, *Brunfelsia calycina macrantha*, with fragrant violet-purple blooms, and *Cassia corymbosa*, a shrubby species bearing racemes of rich yellow flowers.

Before leaving this area, the visitor is strongly recommended to wander around the outside bays between the various glasshouses – in these sheltered spots there are often treasures to be found – at this time of year, for example, there are very good nerines in one place. Other interesting autumn-flowering bulbs include the intergeneric hybrids *Amarcrinum memoria-corsii* and *Amarygia parkeri*, with the elegant *Crinum moorei*, one of the parents of the hardy *Crinum x powelli*. There is also a magnificent plant of the late-flowering, hardy, *Impatiens tinctoria*, native of the mountains of Ethiopia and Kenya, a robust and long-lived perennial.

Strongylodon macrobotrys, the Jade Vine, a fantastic climber from the Philippines, flowers in summer in the warm section of the display glasshouse. The inflorescence is about 70 cm long.

The Main Rose Borders

These are colourful for most of September and October, with some vigorous types holding on until November. In October 1988 we particularly noted 'Ralph Tizard', an attractive coral colour, and a new floribunda, 'Matangi', also coral-coloured, neither of which showed any sign of giving up.

From the rose borders, one can pass

A group of carnivorous plants, displayed in a corridor leading from the main display glasshouse.

by Weather Hill Cottage, pausing briefly to look at the peat beds on the way; here *Cyclamen* and Himalayan gentians are to be seen.

Alpine Meadow

The Alpine Meadow is kept closely mown from summer to autumn, and as a result, large numbers of bulbs appear during September and October and can be seen clearly sticking up above the grass. The crocuses, in particular, make a spectacular show; three species are well established here. The rich purple *Crocus nudiflorus* from the Pyrenees is well naturalised in many places. *Crocus speciosus* from the mountains of northern Turkey is also there, with bluer, veined flowers and there are the pale pinky-mauve flowers of *C.kotschyanus*, including in a few places its variety 'Leucopharynx'. The pinker flowers are all Colchicums, crocus-like in flower, but very different in spring with their broad shining leaves, very poisonous because they contain the

drug colchicine, and so are not grazed, in their native land, even by sheep or goats (who will normally eat anything). *Colchicum speciosum* and its hybrids are best for the open garden, and benefit from rich feeding during early summer and spring. The best I have ever seen were growing in a small enclosure near a barn in the mountains above Trebizond. All the grass had been eaten and the ground had a liberal top dressing of pure cow manure. Here the only plants that had survived were docks and *Colchicum* and both were magnificent.

In damp places among the grass in the alpine meadow the tiny bellflower, *Wahlenbergia hederifolia,* is naturalised, or is perhaps truly native. It is rare in eastern England, but common in the West Country, especially on Dartmoor or Exmoor. The wiry stems creep through the grass, ending in pale blue bells. Along the top of the meadow are planted a number of large Japanese maples. Many cultivars have been selected in Japan for their different leaf

A drift of Crocus nudiflorus *in the Alpine Meadow.*

shapes; the large-growing variety 'Ozakazuki', known for over a hundred years, is consistently one of the best for red colour in autumn – all the leaves tend to turn the same shade of bright red. The leaves may be fifteen centimetres across, and the tree finally reaches about six metres high; in contrast the 'Moon Maple', *Acer japonicum*, which is in the same area, has leaves which become multicoloured, in shades of red, yellow and green, depending on how much sun they receive.

Rock Garden

Although the Rock Garden is probably primarily thought of as a spring attraction, it is in fact full of small treasures which can be enjoyed throughout the year. To prove the point, Ken Aslet, then Superintendent of the Rock Garden, told the audience at a lecture he gave in September 1969 that he had picked a hundred and twenty-nine different kinds of flower in bloom

on the Rock Garden the previous day, and seventy-two in the Alpine House. We are not sure whether or not this experiment has been repeated recently, but invite visitors to try it (*looking* not picking, please!) for themselves to see what today's total is. On a warm day the Himalayan autumn-flowering gentians such as *G.sino-ornata* and its hybrids will be a spectacular sight, forming sheets of blue trumpets with green-striped throats.

Wild Garden

This area, the oldest part of the Garden, was described in some detail in an earlier section (see page 78); although it is at its most spectacular during the late winter and spring, there are a few interesting plants to be seen here during the autumn also. One of these is x *Gaulnettya* 'Wisley Pearl', which is covered with purple berries in the autumn. It is a hybrid between *Pernettya* and *Gaultheria* and flowered for the first

A view towards the laboratory, from the long ponds at the foot of the Rock Garden. Note the bright autumn colour of the Japanese maples in the Alpine Meadow.

117

Fruits of x Gaulnettya *'Wisley Pearl'.*

A colourful display in the Formal Garden; the pale pink flowers are Cleome.

about the end of September *E.x intermedia* bears beautiful flowers of pure white with a central boss of golden stamens, shown off to good effect by the dark green leaves.

The Formal and Walled Gardens

This area was fully described on page 105 of the summer section, but there is still much to be seen during the autumn. Being near the Laboratory and the restaurant, it is a popular part of the Garden, and also has the advantage of being easily accessible to those in wheelchairs. (For details of the suggested routes around the garden for visitors in wheelchairs, enquire at the Information Centre at the entrance to the Garden. A number of wheelchairs are available on loan to disabled visitors – it is advisable to reserve these in advance). During the autumn a new bedding scheme comes into full flower in the formal garden (see below), and in the adjacent walled garden many of the shrubs and herbaceous plants are still in

time in the Wild Garden in 1929. Also of interest are the Eucryphias, surely some of the most beautiful shrubs and trees to be found in English gardens; amongst those to be seen here are two good specimens of *Eucryphia* x *intermedia*, an evergreen hybrid between *E.glutinosa* and *E.lucida*. From the end of August to

full bloom. Roses, once again, can be relied on to provide a good show almost until Christmas- for example 'Tour de Malakoff', a large bush with huge bright pink flowers, 'Coral Dawn', a climber with pale pink blossoms, and 'Ballerina', a small single – flowered bybrid musk, should be worth seeing in October and November.

One group of annual and herbaceous plants that keep their colour well into September, and sometimes October, is *Centaurea*, of which the best known is probably the cornflower, *C.cyanus*. In the walled garden, however, is another representative of the family – *C.* 'John Coutts', with lovely rose-pink, yellow-centred flowers; this is a variety of *C.dealbata*, a species from the Caucasus and Iran.

Outside the walled garden there is a narrow border, which, backed as it is by a south-facing wall, makes a comfortable home for a number of sun-loving or slightly tender plants. Notable here in autumn are two rare colchicums – *Colchicum laetum* and *C.cilicicum*. The latter is a native of southern Turkey in the foothills of the Taurus mountains, where it grows among rocks and on scree – hence its love of sunny, well-drained soil. It produces its rather small, bright pink blooms from September to November. *C.laetum* is very different, having many pale pink, narrow-petalled flowers; this species was originally described from S.Russia, although there is some doubt as to the country of origin of many of the cultivated plants.

Seven Acres

Seven Acres contains a number of trees and shrubs that are spectacular in the autumn. Perhaps the most immediately striking is the fine, relatively young specimen of *Nyssa sylvatica* (see above), which turns brilliant red and orange every year. A native of eastern North America, where it thrives in swampy situations, *N.sylvatica* was introduced into this country during the early part of the eighteenth century; here it does well on ordinary soil, and rewards the gardener with brilliantly coloured foliage in autumn. Nearby is another

finely-coloured tree, *Liquidambar styraciflua*, also from damp ground in the eastern USA; this tree has been known in English gardens for longer than the *Nyssa*, as it was introduced here in the seventeenth century. The specimen in Seven Acres was measured in 1964, and was then twenty-five metres high, with a girth of two metres; it is still growing, and may be expected

This specimen of Nyssa sylvatica *in Seven Acres never fails to colour spectacularly.*

Hard graft! A tree trunk path being laid next to the Round Pond.

The Round Pond in Seven Acres: on the far bank can be seen the huge leaves of Gunnera manicata; *next to it is* Taxodium distichum.

Zelkova cretica *in Seven Acres.*

to reach about 30m. The maple-like leaves turn purple, and then red, and a sweet-smelling resin is produced, giving rise to the common name 'sweet gum'. Near these is a fine pair of Metasequoias, which turn a good reddish-brown in autumn, and can be compared with the *Taxodium* on the island of the same lake.

Heather Garden

Some people feel that heathers are fine on a moor, but that one can have too much of them in a garden. That said, the reason that heathers can sometimes look so unsatisfactory in the garden is because they are planted in patches of a single colour, dotted about in a mish-mash of colours, often with different species adjacent to one another; this produces a totally unnatural effect. The most successful plantings of heathers that we have ever seen have worked because the plants have been grown in very large drifts of the same species, but with the different colours blended together – giving a more natural effect. Large groups of different species can also be blended together so that the flowering period in that area is extended.

The Heather Garden at Wisley is no exception to this, and is especially attractive in those areas where the plants have grown into, and through, one another (and where there are also taller specimens to add variety). It also has the benefit of being large, with the result that it is possible to grow good large clumps of the tall tree heathers which are valuable for both height, flower colour in spring and rich, feathery foliage. Having said all this, we now have to tell you that a new Heather Garden is in the process of being planted on Howards Field, and in due course the present garden will be phased out – so, make the most of it while it is there for you to enjoy!

The Heather Garden was first made in the 1920's after F.J. Chittenden, Director of the Laboratory and Garden, had spotted small plants of ling (*Calluna vulgaris*) growing on Seven Acres, an area previously considered unsuitable

for any kind of cultivation. This original Heather Garden has been altered and improved over the years, being almost entirely replanted during the late 1960's. The present Heather Garden is at its best from late July until October, although there are features of interest here throughout the year. The collection occupies a number of curving beds, and amongst the heaths and heathers are a group of Scots pines and a number of smaller trees including birches, rowans, dwarf conifers and junipers.

During the autumn some of our native species and their garden forms are particularly notable; *Erica cinerea*, the bell heather, and its late-flowering cultivars, such as 'Cindy' and 'Cevennes' make a fine show, as do 'Mrs D.F. Maxwell' and 'Valerie Proudley' – both forms of the Cornish heath *Erica vagans*. *Daboecia cantabrica*, the Irish bell heather, flowers almost continuously here, even though the conditions are very different to the damp heathland of its homeland, Connemara. *Calluna vulgaris*, mentioned above, is a very varied species, showing a wide range of flower

The lake in Seven Acres; this photograph was taken rather later in the autumn than the picture opposite.

The Heather Garden in Seven Acres; in the background is a fine specimen of Parrotia persica.

and foliage colours; more than seventy different cultivars of this species are grown in the Heather Garden, and they provide the main display in September and October. Nearby, on a mound to the north of the lake, is a collection of slow-growing and dwarf conifers, presented to the Society by Mr A.H. Nisbet. The largest have now reached about five metres, and show an interesting diversity of colour and botanical origin. Some have retained their original congested or prostrate form, whilst others, such as *Abies procera* 'Glauca prostrata', have reverted to the original form; this is shooting skywards as if to make up time to form the fifty-metre tree it can become even in this country (in California it can reach about eighty metres).

We mentioned above that the heather collection is about to be transferred to a new site in Howards Field, so this seems to be a good place to mention the new Propagation and Research Department that was set up during 1988. A new glasshouse and a number of growing bays were constructed to provide improved facilities for propagating and growing on the many thousands of plants required to replace those destroyed in the storm, and also for new developments, such as the heather collection, which, it is hoped, will include around twenty-eight thousand heathers. The new heather garden will in fact become the National Heather Collection, under the scheme for national collections run by the NCCPG (see page 80), and, as such, should be of considerable interest.

Those who patronise the restaurant will be rewarded not only with the most delicious food, but also with an extremely good view of the beds of red hot pokers, *Kniphofia*, over by the Round Pond. These striking plants come from South Africa, where they often grow in thousands in marshy fields and by streams in damp ground. They hybridise easily, and many cultivars have

been raised, such as 'Orangeman' and 'Royal Standard', both large and strongly coloured. Also to be seen from the restaurant are the beds of Ornamental Grasses. One of the great strengths of the grass family is that the elegant form and structure of the individual plant is attractive and valuable in the garden. Many of them make large clumps and are particularly suitable for planting at the back of a border, although there are also a number of dwarf forms which can be used to good effect in the front of a mixed border, or in association with paving or gravel paths. Amongst the many species and cultivars to be seen here is *Miscanthus sinensis* 'Silver Feather'. which keeps its fluffy reed-like seed heads into winter. Pampas grasses (*Cortaderia* species) are well-represented here also, with three forms of *C.selloana* – 'Pumila', 'Sunningdale Silver' and 'Rendatleri', at ten feet the tallest, and with its pinkish plumes probably the most beautiful of all.

A pair of fastigiate hornbeams frame this view from Howards Field, looking towards the Pinetum. The new Heather Garden is situated near here.

A group of the red hot poker, Kniphofia *'Royal Standard', in a bed near the Round Pond.*

Borders by formal pool

Peonies, *Gypsophila* and summer bedding are the dominant plants in this area, but there is also a large group of the late-flowering *Perovskia atriplicifolia* from the steppes of Central Asia. Its greyish, deeply-cut leaves and tall lavender-purple spikes of small flowers are most attractive.

Some of the shrubs in this area are still to be found in flower during the autumn – notably the roses, for example 'Dove', one of David Austin's well-known English roses, which has wonderful pinky-apricot flowers. Incidentally, one of 'Dove's' parents is 'Wife of Bath', with shell-pink flowers – she should be still in flower by the restaurant. At the back of these beds are two trees noted for their autumn colour; *Cercidiphyllum japonicum*, whose golden leaves smell of burnt jam in the autumn, and the low-growing *Parrotia persica* with flaking bark and variously-coloured leaves.

The Seed Department

One of the privileges available to members of the Society is that of participating in the Society's surplus seed distribution programme. Every year two full-time, and three part-time staff send out over 200,000 packets of seed to members and botanic gardens (over 250 of them) all over the world. Most of the seed is collected, cleaned and labelled at Wisley, although a few members, especially those who live abroad, also donate small quantities of particularly interesting seed. As Howard Dixon, Head of the Department, mentioned in an article on the subject in *The Garden*, "If members, on walking round the Garden, see a person, head down, fumbling in the plants, they are not necessarily helping themselves to plant material – it may be one of our department collecting seed. Perhaps we ought to have some method of identification on our hindquarters!"

Right
Early morning in Seven Acres.

Below
The plan for the Formal Canal, Walled and Formal Gardens (see page 37).

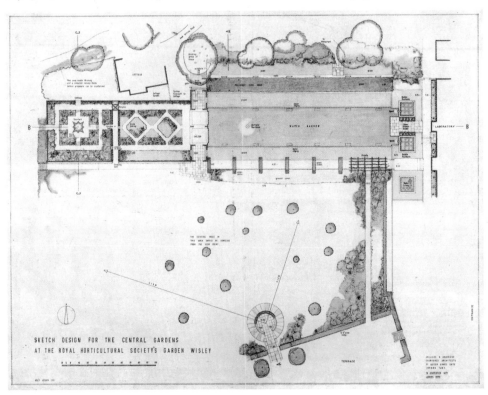

Index

Bold type indicates illustration

The benefits of belonging to the Royal Horticultural Society

Your own copy of the Society's journal 'The Garden' every month

As soon as you become a member of the Society, you can look forward to receiving your first copy of 'The Garden'.

Long recognised as the leading magazine for horticulturists and gardeners, 'The Garden' will develop your knowledge of horticulture through in-depth articles and will keep you in touch with news and current affairs in the gardening world.

Special tickets for Chelsea Flower Show

Members of the RHS have priority when booking special tickets to the Chelsea Flower Show, which is held in the last full week of May each year. For the special days reserved for RHS members and their guests on 23rd and 24th May, tickets are just £8 (reduced to £6 for 3pm to 8pm). Normal tickets cost £14 (1989 prices).

To ensure that your ticket reservation is secured, a priority form will be sent with your membership pack as soon as we receive your application to join the Society.

Free tickets for Shows and Demonstrations throughout the year

Our members enjoy free entry to the Society's Shows and lectures each month at our Westminster Halls.

Your membership also entitles you to free entry to more than 40 lectures and demonstrations arranged by the Society throughout the British Isles.

Free visits to some of the best gardens in the World

Our members can enjoy unlimited free visits with a guest to the RHS Gardens at Wisley in Surrey and Rosemoor in Devon throughout the year.

We have also arranged free entry for our members to the beautiful gardens at Harlow Car near Harrogate, Ness in the Wirral, Hidcote Manor in Gloucestershire, Bodnant in North Wales, and Sheffield Park and Nymans in Sussex.

To make the most of Wisley or Rosemoor frequently, you might like to buy an additional season card for £6 which allows you to take two extra guests into these gardens at any time.

Advice on your gardening problems

A very important part of the Society's work is the advisory service we offer members, who may consult a specific expert on any gardening problem.

This service is completely free to our members.

Take advantage of surplus seed offers from Wisley Garden

Each year our garden at Wisley has extra seeds which we are pleased to offer to our members, free except for a small postage and packing charge.

Borrow books from the world-famous Lindley Library

As a UK member you have unlimited access to the best horticultural library in the world.

You may borrow books or enjoy hours of quiet research and fact finding whenever you like.

How to join the RHS Application for membership should be made to:

The Secretary
The Royal Horticultural Society
PO Box 313
Vincent Square
London SW1P 2PE